HOW TO INVEST IN RENTAL PROPERTIES FOR BEGINNERS

(The Guide for Passive Income)

BY

Lisa Turner - Brandon Phillips

© COPYRIGHT 2019 BY DE

LISA TURNER – BRANDON PHILLIPS

ALL RIGHTS RESERVED.

This document is geared towards providing exact and reliable information with regard to the topic and issue covered. The publication is sold with the idea that the publisher is not required to render accounting, officially permitted, or otherwise, qualified services. If advice is necessary, legal or professional, a practiced individual in the profession should be addressed.

From a Declaration of Principles which was accepted and approved equally by a Committee of the American Bar Association and a Committee of Publishers and Associations.

In no way is it legal to reproduce, duplicate, or transmit any part of this document in either electronic means or in printed format. Recording of this publication is strictly prohibited and any storage of this document is not allowed unless with written permission from the publisher. All rights reserved.

The information provided herein is stated to be truthful and consistent, in that any liability, in terms of inattention or otherwise, by any usage or abuse of any policies, processes, or directions contained within is the solitary and utter responsibility of the recipient reader. Under no circumstances will any legal responsibility or blame be held against the publisher for any reparation, damages, or monetary loss due to the information herein, either directly or indirectly.

Respective authors own all copyrights not held by the publisher.

The information herein is offered solely for informational purposes and is universal as so. The presentation of the information is without a contract or any type of guarantee assurance.

The trademarks that are used are without any consent, and the publication of the trademark is without permission or backing by the trademark owner. All trademarks and brands within this book are for clarifying purposes only and are owned by the owners themselves, not affiliated with this document.

Disclaimer

All erudition contained in this book is given for informational and educational purposes only. The author is not in any way accountable for any result or outcomes that emanate from using this material. Constructive attempts have been made to provide information that is both accurate and effective, but the author is not bound for the accuracy or use/misuse of this information.

Foreword

First, I will like to thank you for taking the first step of trusting me and deciding to purchase/read this life-transforming eBook. Thanks for spending your time and resources on this material.

I can assure you of exact results if you will diligently follow the exact blueprint, I lay bare in the information manual you are currently reading. It has transformed lives, and I strongly believe it will equally transform your own life too.

All the information I presented in this Do It Yourself piece is easy to digest and practice.

Contents

INTRODUCTION 1

CHAPTER ONE 16

WHAT'S RENTAL PROPERTIES 16

CHAPTER TWO 68

WHAT'S A INCOME PASSIVE 68

CHAPTER THREE 95

Important things to note while embarking on a Rental property business 95

CHAPTER FOUR 117

Analyzing a rental property 117

CHAPTER FIVE 136

How to set the right price for your Rental property listing 136

INTRODUCTION

Today we're divulging Rental property Adventures – an improvement of Rental property Experiences that incorporates the thinking boggling open door for challenging visitors to channel their inward Phileas Fogg and tour Around the World in Eighty Days. This epic voyage crosswise over six of the Earth's landmasses joins exceptional Adventures now on hand to book through hosts on Rental property extending from following lions via strolling with Sabache Warriors in Kenya to chasing for UFOs with Nate in Arizona.

Since there has been a significant drop in the charges for Rental property, the manageable commissions that Rental property professionals and intermediaries could gather have additionally dropped. In any case, the drop in commissions can be more than counterbalanced by the measure of homes that can be sold. What's more, getting first-rate Rental property leads is one of the keys to making this a reality for Rental property experts. This is on the grounds that there is such a widespread quantity of a better wide variety of houses available now than there have been earlier than the air pocket blasted.

The ascent in the extent of property holders who are submerged on their home loans has increased so much that an extraordinarily huge range of them have concluded that they cannot continue living in their homes. They would pick to sell their home and purchase a comparable domestic at a tons lower cost, and anticipate the misfortune with the purpose that they can improve their profits circumstance through having a lower contract installment each and every month. What's more, considering there is no deficiency of properties to purchase, these men and women had no difficulty finding a practical home at a decent cost.

Also, any other after effect of the ascent in accessible houses is that an ever-growing number of individuals are ending up first-time property holders. Since prices on homes are falling, an ever-growing number of individuals can manipulate the cost of a domestic for a similar sum they are at present paying in lease. So the clever choice for these men and women is to purchase a house as averse to intending to lease.

These factors surely lead to one thing- a better sized requirement for Rental property operators to support the buying and promoting of these properties. In this manner, no matter the truth that expenses have fallen, the amount of reachable properties, purchasers, and merchants has increased which more than compensates at the lower prices involving how much a given Rental property operator may want to make in the modern-day Rental property advertise. What's more, as we all know, the more clients a Rental property operator has, the more properties they will promote and the more cash they will make.

The difficulty, however, comes when a Rental property professional has skilled their current client list. The best route for them to get more customers is to get more Rental property leads one way or the other. In addition to the reality that they need more leads, they need awesome leads on the off chance that they will be high quality in altering over a high variety of them into clients who genuinely finish on purchasing as nicely as selling at least one property.

So how can you get greater Rental property leads? There is obviously a wide range of methods. These include getting them from a company that offers them, promoting, shopping for in to lead age sites, developing and preserving present-day Rental property web site that draws conceivable

customers to it, and try to get them all of via your personal system. There are quite a number of specific techniques for creating Rental property leads too, but these are the most extensively diagnosed strategies - all of which have proven to work in a specific way.

Perhaps the most ordinary strategy to get Rental property leads is with the aid of buying them. There are groups whose sole intention is to discover people who want to purchase or sell a property. They at that point provide this information to people who are eager to pay for it. So in the match that you are a Rental property professional searching for Rental property leads and do not have the probability to locate your own, or you actually would choose not to do it now, at that point this might be a first-rate desire for you.

There are two different ways to go about this. You can purchase the Rental property leads from an organization as a lot of information that you will get as a rundown or spreadsheet. At that point, you have to start filtering through them and making use of the information reachable to qualify and arrange them yourself. What's more, from that factor forward, it is an ideal possibility to start making inquiries into finding out if they are reliable leads or not.

The other method for obtaining Rental property leads is via shopping in a Rental property lead generator site that will send you a lot of littler preparations of leads all the time. This can be respectable in terms of the reality that the information is in all likelihood going to be considerably greater existing than purchasing a solitary extraordinarily considerable rundown of leads. In any case, this also implies that there is less to work with so it would not provide you a great deal opportunity related to choosing who to contact first.

Obtaining Rental property leads or shopping in a lead age site can likewise be costly. This can be a terrible element considering the fact that the whole goal of buying leads is to find out customers, promote properties, and make commissions if the leads that you purchase do not change into commissions. All things considered, not only did you not sell any residences (or several properties), but you squandered money on vain data, and you sat around idly following clueless leads when you could have been taking a shot at discovering awesome Rental property leads.

Another strategy to produce Rental property leads is with the aid of publicizing. On the off risk that you are a Rental property operator, dealer, or agent, advertising your administrations might be a good opportunity to find serious Rental property leads. This kind of lead is amazing because rather than going through the stress of seeking folks who want to buy or promote a property, the tables are turned and they come searching for you.

Notwithstanding, having individuals strive to find you rather than you trying to find them, there is another advantage to publicizing to create Rental property leads. The people who are trying to find you are mostly serious people who have property they want to purchase or sell. This implies that you do not want to stress over whether or not they are going to end up being certified leads or not because they will actually be.

A related technique to produce Rental property leads by means of merchandising which can be appreciably more potential than essentially publicizing on a bulletin or in the paper is via putting up your very own Rental property site. Sites are shockingly economical to have facilitated, and having one created for you does not need to be costly either. What's more, in the match that you obtain skill ability with the fundamentals of website improvement, you will have the option to maintain it except absolutely everyone else's enter after it is been set up so you can commonly keep it current.

The importance of keeping your website up-to-date cannot be downplayed. To start with, you want to maintain it refreshed with the homes you are attempting to promote so the persons who visit your web page will have something to take a gander at - and considering this rundown of properties will change as your consumer rundown develops and transforms, you will have to trade your website frequently to be a part of the new residences and dispose of the ones that are never n longer accessible.

Another reason why you should keep your web site refreshed all the time is because it will help your page rank grow. Web indexes utilize certain factors to decide that they are so pertinent to specific catchphrases, and the place to show them in a rundown of question items. Also, probably the greatest thing that pushes a website online towards the easiest priority on the rundown is its web page rank, which is highly influenced by means of how dynamic and how contemporary the site is. So typically, the more you update your site, the greater its web page rank will be, and the more it's going to show up in question objects recognized with Rental property catchphrases, and the extra guests you'll get to your site.

When you bring friends to your site, you may be getting the presentation you need to conceivable clients for free. They can stay on your website online for as long as they need to and take a gander at few or the wide variety of houses as they want to. What's more, you do not want to do anything so as to help them. Indeed there might be a massive wide variety of men and women all on your web page simultaneously. That is something that you would now not possibly ever have the threat to do face to face. This marvel is what is regarded as an influence, and affect is the component that can radically change a personal mission into a fortune 500 business pretty right now when overseen effectively.

The most ideal method to do Rental property lead age likewise happens to have a lot of challenges - in any tournament initially. Another strategy for discovering leads is by using shape a big system and utilizing it. This is probably the most perfect techniques to get leads on the grounds that it is one of the most shockingly compelling ways. Be that as it may, lamentably, it is likewise one of the most difficult techniques to begin and requires a full-size stretch of time to yield results.

The primary thing you need to do is to commence assembling your system. What's more, it isn't too big that you need to begin constructing it; you have to deliberately listen on shape your machine every end every day, regardless of your location or who you are talking to, this is on the grounds that for wonderful many people, organizing would not work out easily.

In the event that you resemble notable many people, you are most possibly to some degree timid and don't make it a point to deliberately meet and converse with new people all the time. Be that as it may, on the off chance that you need to construct a system, you may want to do precisely that. This is something that can come as a test no doubt, both virtually and actually, then again it is sincerely justified even no matter the exertion over the long haul.

It could possibly be difficult in mild of the reality that a big piece of the structure and a substantial machine is managing dismissal. What's more, on the off hazard that you want to collect a tremendous system rapidly, you may want to manage an extraordinary deal of dismissal each and every single day. Such a large range of individuals, being rejected is taken with the aid of and by and it winds up carrying them out with the intention that they give up quite too early before the benefits that constructing a huge gadget gives comes. In any case, if you are able to pull through and not give up easily, you may be successful where others failed and surrendered.

Furthermore, structures administration to produce Rental property leads be possible anyplace. When you have to fuel your vehicle, go away on the contrary facet of the siphon from any individual who's as of now there and attempt to start up a discussion the place you may have the option to disclose to them that you are in the Rental property business and can help them or any other individual they realize who would possibly hope to buy or sell. What's more, in case you're extraordinarily proper about it, you may need to just get $10 or some other restrained extent of gasoline one after any other so you will have to go to the corner shop all the greater often and have greater chances to arrange.

You can also construct your system with the aid of gathering new people at some other spot. You may want to speak with any person at the market, library, church, keeping up in line at the bank, or anyplace you are around other men and women for in excess of a couple of minutes one after some other and establishing a discussion wouldn't be excessively ungainly. It tends to be performed anyplace, with distinctly a good deal anybody, at practically whenever. Also, the more dedicated you are to it, the quicker you will have the choice to advance your system and the happier you will be over the long haul.

Probably the most perfect tactics to the community are via conversing with the persons you definitely know. These are individuals who are as of now in your system, and you can use them to enable you boost your system. The most evident route is to just inquire as to whether or not they are eager to purchase or sell a property quicker as a substitute than later, and to bear in mind that you are available to help them.

However, every other approach to allow you to strengthen your gadget is to ask them who they comprehend that would possibly be keen on buying or selling a property. You are really drawing close to them for Rental property leads using a range of words. You ought to method them for the names and portions of men and women who they recognize who might be keen on buying or selling a property, or you should request that they provide your contact facts to the men and women they have at the pinnacle of the precedence list when you ask them that inquiry.

It's important to always have your business cards with your contact information correctly updated on them when you are organizing these conversations. That way you may not want to rely on individuals' recollections which are truly now not the most stable things when contrasted with something they can basically peruse from a card. Cards then again make it so the man or woman you are giving your contact records to would not want to depend on their memory, and it advances a steadily professional image also which can simply earnings you.

Rental property traits have taken a leap and one of the effects it has brought on are many. A lot more homes are reachable in modern times compared to when the economic system took a make a plunge 2008. This implies that despite the reality that the costs are lower, the higher amount of houses reachable make it possible to buy and promote a greater quantity and make greater money in commissions consequently which will greater than compensate for the diminished character property estimations.

Ten years prior, a quest for Rental property would have begun in the neighborhood as the place of business or driving around town. At the operator's office, you would go through an early evening time flipping through pages of dynamic property postings from the close by Multiple Listing Service (MLS). In the wake of picking houses of intrigue, you would spend several weeks traveling each and every property till you located the right one. Discovering market information to empower you to survey the asking cost would take extra time and significantly more driving, notwithstanding, you probably might not have the option to discover the majority of the data you expected to get extraordinarily alright with an equitable worth.

CHAPTER ONE

WHAT'S RENTAL PROPERTIES

With respect to rental land, promoting a rental home, screening and picking inhabitants and managing speculation, properties should generally be given up over to capable property executive or property board association. In any case, there are those of you land budgetary masters out there who, like me, the value is actually connected with each piece of your speculation properties. Similarly, like some of you, I have before long managed my course of action of speculation properties for a long time now. The three biggest troubles I have kept running into has been suitably exhibiting my rental homes, picking the right occupants and managing the owner tenant associations. In this three-area, three-month course of action, I will talk about all of the three challenges and offer a couple of suggestions and insight to empower you to successfully manage tenant turnover and your rental homes feasibly.

Consistently, I have made sense of how to dependably apply a particular game plan of goals and criteria which have helped me keep up a turnover opening pace of under 30 days for each venture property and a typical residency of 3 years. Moreover, my tenants have always revered my rental homes that I have never had to hold any piece of a security store. The present month's article bases on the four essential objectives to consider in successfully advancing your rental homes.

Research rhythmic movement rental rates in your general region. Most importantly, you have to keep up with the rental rates in your general region. Maybe the best slip up owners cause isn't to totally go about asking what the market rental rates are in their general region. Various landowners simply demand the proportional or a slightly higher rent than what their last tenant was paying. This technique, especially in the present land promote, doesn't, for the most part, reflect the heading that the local market has gone in. Thus, you have to conduct your own investigation. Start on the web and see what others are charging for properties like yours. Most venture properties are not advertised on the web so you will need to become progressively familiar with your neighborhood. Starting from the area your speculation property is located in, you should end up being totally aware of what each and every home charge for rent and what the asking rent is.

Call each and every home for rent sign you see and chat with the owner or property executive. Approach them and find out what they are requesting lease and ask them what substantial explanation. Asking generally will give you free information with respect to the close-by market. On a couple of occasions, I have called a property boss curious about the rent and have found that, for example, their property has been accessible for 90 days and rental prospects seem, by all accounts, to be in the $1,100 region. Having that sort of information is important for reducing the length of a chance. If you have no equal houses for rent in your area expand your interest to other places around. Take a 5-mile range and drive around and see how much various homes are for rent in that area. The more research you do, the more calls you make, the more exact your awareness of the going industry division rate in your general region will be.

Set your rent at a forceful level. When you understand that the asking rent in your speculation property's zone is maybe $1100 to $1300, you need to understand what your asking rent will be. Obviously, you have to get much for your property as could sensibly be normal. In any case, you would lean toward not to widen your opening more than it ought to be. You should also have the alternative to reveal to a prospective occupant why you are asking what you are asking. If you have done your investigation early, you should have no issue reacting to those requests. Avoid the temptation to set the rent based on what your home credit portion is. Your home advance portion has little to do with the rental market in your general region. A better technique to set the rent is by taking a typical of what all intents and purposes indistinguishable speculation properties asking rent is for.

Along the line if there are 4 properties in your subdivision that are really or almost like your rental, comparably flowed some place in the scope of $1,100 and $1,300, an extraordinary asking rent would apparently be around $1,200. I said "around" in light of the fact that everyone likes to feel like they have gotten it. You likely need to ask hardly above what you are really planning to get. In our hypothetical circumstance, that might be $1,225 or $1,250. Your goal here isn't to be subsequently banned from the idea by your rental prospects with the complaint that yours is the most exorbitant rental in the zone. You, on the other hand, should try not to give the property away too cheaply. This typical rental rate approach has worked and is still working well for me.

Start publicizing your rental at any rate 30 days out. When you understand what the going rental rates are in your rental's subdivision or zone, it's an incredible chance to begin publicizing. Ideally, you should explore your close by market rents and start publicizing your home rental on any occasion 30 days, anyway in a perfect world 60, going before your anticipated opening. The best spot to begin publicizing is by advertising on home rentals advertising destinations. Let me state that, rental prospects glancing through online are commonly driving their interests 30 to 60 days out from their anticipated move date. Getting a head start by advancing on the web is essential. As arranged occupants are heading off to the web progressively more to begin their mission for a venture property and the introduction the web offers is really what you need to start. Your advancing arrangement cannot stop there nonetheless.

I have found that from 30 days going before your anticipated opening to 30 days into your chance, a great deal of the leaseholder asks to begin from rental prospects driving the zone searching for homes for rent. Anyone driving in your property's neighborhood ought to understand that your property is for rent and they need to easily find how to contact you. Your property's signage should be decipherable and placed in significantly angles of your property where they are easily seen. The asks and leads delivered by signs on your venture property should be similar to the ones made by online advertisements. That is the explanation your course of action should combine.

Hold Open House on parts of the bargains. Let's face it. No one needs to experience their parts of the bargains believing that prospective tenants will pound on the door. In any case, holding an open house is an unfathomably convincing way to deal with exhibit your property to everyone that is interested during a profitable window of time. You can advertise your open house on the web and crash the need to make special trips out to your property to exhibit it to one individual who may can't avoid being may not show up. Open houses in like manner let you converse with arranged tenants eye to eye and "sell" your rental home's features even more effectively. Seeing your prospective tenants in person is significantly more convincing than overview pictures on the web. Something different I like about open houses is that they help me "change" my perception of the rental market by empowering me to chat with various pending occupants briefly.

That causes me to see firsthand what the market extent of the people coming through really is. Everything considered, if my investigation shows that a sensible asking rent is $1,200, yet every prospect that I chat with is looking for something in the $1,000 range, that will offer me a really conventional hint that my asking rent is probably still a bit too high. Finally, open houses can be amazing. I have done open houses for all of my properties every Saturday and Sunday until I have found the right occupants. In addition, half of my occupants found my property through the yard sign they saw during my open house.

When you combine concentrated research and locating the best advertisements arrangement, you can definitely increase the length of your home rental chances. I have been sticking to this procedure for a long time presently to find occupants for my properties. The industrious work I put in has continually paid off. I have reliably had the choice to find occupants in less than 30 days. The direction is clear. Make your advancing arrangement having these four goals in mind and tail it. You will be satisfied with the results.

Different people wish to rent their property. A vacant property could quickly change into a budgetary channel and may cause significant issues. Convincing, publicizing is a response for such a circumstance, which can help in fixing off the unoccupied units.

Different ways are there to exhibit your speculation property. The factors that should be considered while picking a procedure to advance your property are the size of the speculation property and whether you have to pay for publicizing it. If it is just a room or part of the house, you probably won't want to pay for advertisement. In any case, for a greater unit publicizing winds up fundamental. There are useful systems that could empower you to deliver heaps of potential thought for your speculation property.

Paid Advertising

When going for paid advertisement the essential task is to wear down the publicizing plan that will help the appearance of publicizing theory similarly as acknowledge potential leaseholders. First of all, you need to show where your property is located. If it is located in a nearby street, you should pitch in the local paper or buy advertisement space on destinations including close-by business information.

Do make reference to what makes your speculation property stand separated than the rest like a pool or a mind-blowing view. Despite whether your property isn't extraordinary, you can find a part that would address the occupants and outfit them with a settlement, for instance, an incredible neighborhood, a near to strip mall or an open transportation space.

You need to understand your local market so that you can offer forceful rates to beat the test. You could isolate from the leasing strategy that is balanced in your general region. For example, if the property owners in your general region offer a year or longer leases, you could offer a month-to-month lease, a similar number of leaseholders don't support denoting a whole deal contract.

Use the verbal. Request that your satisfied inhabitants share extraordinary information about your property and thusly, you could offer them pioneers charge for their referrals. You could in like manner use 'For Rent' signs.

Non-Paid Advertising

To begin with, you need to partner to accomplish this goal. You can let your family, partners, and colleagues consider the property you wish to put on rent. They can imply a potential customer to you. You will be astonished by how much ideas you can get from this source. In addition, you can post flyers of your property on notice loads up. You can also post fliers at your workplace or your friend's workplace. You can also visit your Local High Commission site and get your property enlisted. They would not charge you anything. You can similarly post free commercials at locales that grant them.

The most helpful move to make is to put a 'For Rent' sign outside your speculation property. You can also put the number of rooms and washrooms available close to your contact number. By giving these little details, those people will call you who are very charmed and you would save yourself the cerebral agony of giving everybody nuances.

Arriving at speculation property estimation value is a noteworthy business for land budgetary masters and all others busy with land contributing. Since picking the right estimation of venture property - paying little heed to whether as a seller or buyer - can be the qualification between assumption advantage and incident.

This is the explanation speculation property estimation assessments are reliably the result of wide research and exhaustive land assessment that enable one to really jump into the property's budgetary introduction. Sensible enough.

Coincidentally, it's not always sensible to do wide figuring and a portion of the time all that is called for is a quick strategy to for the most part assess what a venture property cost should be as a first-look assessment reliant on insignificant data.

So in this article, we're going to look at four tallies you can quickly process with not more than a pad and pencil when you need to quickly decide what a make speculation property is worth.

As you will see, every one of the four techniques requires some data about late speculation property development in your close-by market. Regardless, that isn't extremely difficult to get - especially in the event that you're generous with an appraiser or someone adequately attracted to land contributing.

It should be noted that all of the four methodologies fused into two plans; One that discloses to you the best approach to calculate the estimation itself, and one that demonstrates to you the best approach to use the estimation to register property estimation.

Value Per Unit

Cost per unit concerns the number of rentable units the property offers. It is a respectable strategy to make speculation property estimation checks since it's helpful yet easy to use.

Worth Per Unit = Asking Price/Number of Units

Property Value = Number of Units x Price Per Unit

Worth Per Square Foot

Worth per square foot has to do with the structure's zone. For this part, it will, in general, either reflect the account for the gross structure and area or the physical space that the occupant includes (i.e., the units). Our plans concern gross structure area yet it works a comparison when it applies to units.

Worth Per Square Foot = Property Value/Square Footage of Improvements

Property Value = Square Footage of Improvements x Price Per Square Foot

Gross Rent Multiplier

Gross rent multiplier (or GRM) has for quite a while been used via land theorists as a speedy and straightforward way to deal with venture property estimation checks. This method concerns the property's cash related execution (i.e., net arranged pay).

Gross Rent Multiplier = Property Value/Gross Scheduled Income

Property Value = Gross Scheduled Income x Gross Rent Multiplier

Top Rate

Top rate (or capitalization rate) is the most outstanding (and perhaps the best) way to deal with speculation property estimation measures, anyway, it requires cash related data about a venture property that might be more elusive than the data required for the past strategies since you would need to determine a speculation property's net compensation to make the calculation - and that information could be instantly open.

Top Rate = Net Operating Income/Property Value

Property Value = Net Operating Income/Cap Rate

Principle concern

Every one of the four procedures gives a not too bad technique for you to quickly and viably make venture property estimation measures. Clearly, you have to make sure to use strong data. So have a go at doing some investigation in your general region and make a couple of relationships with appraisers or different real estate professionals that you can rely on to provide you with reliable data.

Close to the day's end, be that as it may, your time and effort will be worth the efforts. So it would be sharp for you to start doing some homework.

Speculation property costs are the crucial shades of spite that goes with owning property that you rent out to different people to pay to use. One way to make your money work for you is to buy homes, associations, and properties, which different people will pay you to use. With these properties comes property the administrator's costs.

The most outstanding property the administrator's costs that owners need to pay are the land charges. By far most who guarantee property must cover administrative commitments on that property. The neighborhood, state, and government obligations may apply to the properties that you have.

Keeping up their possessions additionally goes into the property board charges that land proprietors need to pay. Upkeep issues with houses and structures happen normally. In the event that you lease your homes out to other individuals, those individuals expect that you should keep the structures in the best condition. Proprietors are always booking individuals to keep an eye on cooling and warming frameworks. The proprietors need to give a great deal of consideration to the pipes and electrical wiring in the structures they lease to other individuals. The most ideal approach to deal with the upkeep issues is for the landowner to plan standard support by experts.

Investment property expenses include the expense of safeguarding the property. When you buy a bit of property you need to guarantee it to secure the resources you put into it. Regardless of whether you have the ideal inhabitants an inadvertent fire, or a demonstration of Mother Nature, can harm your property. Landowners must keep their possessions secured to guarantee the resources they invested in them. Property owners additionally need protection that will ensure them on the off chance that somebody claims they were harmed on the property they possess.

Investment property expenses likewise, incorporate the charges the landowner pays on the cash they make from letting out the property. These expenses differ, depending on the number of possessions the individual owns, the size of their family, and the reasonings the proprietor might have the option to guarantee on the deterioration of the property.

A large number of individuals claim investment properties contract organizations that deal with the undertakings related to the possessions. These organizations help with things like meeting potential occupants and gather month to month leases, and timetable fixes to the structure. Contracting these organizations to carry out these responsibilities will enable the landowner to have all the more spare time.

In the event that an occupant doesn't pay their rent, the property owner needs to record papers with the court to begin removal. Now and then the landowner needs to indict the occupant to get paid for the monies they owe. These court sessions can cost cash in documenting charges, and lawyer expenses.

Supplanting machines that break is another sort of cost that a few proprietors have to bear. On the off chance that the house that the landowner leases have stoves, high temp water radiators, clothes washers, dryers, forced air systems, warmers, iceboxes, or dishwashers, at that point the property owner should supplant these things every now and then. The majority of these kinds of costs can be utilized as findings when the proprietor documents their own personal tax documents.

In the event that you that obtaining an investment property and leasing it out and gathering is only that simple, you're extremely off-base. In the event that you take a look at it from the point of view of it being an approach to create additional salary then everything looks extraordinary on the grounds that other than the pay from the tenants you may likewise benefit from lodging cost expands that have been going up for many years.

There are disadvantages to being a proprietor of an investment property. Being a landowner is significantly more than simply gathering the lease on the first of every month, consistently. There is genuine lot of work required alongside high money related dangers.

Here are a couple of things to mull over before you take an interest in an investment property. Any investment property is not normal for any main living place; the investment property is a genuine money related venture. When you buy a home it has a greater amount of an enthusiastic angle than a monetary interest in a rental does.

You are a "financial specialist" not simply the proprietor of a property. This implies you need to change your perspective and take a look at this property as far as benefit and misfortune, hazard and reward. There are two fundamental factors that will represent the moment of truth you in this sort of venture, specifically: 1) Cash Flow - you have to think about many leases you can gather for this property consistently, and after that what will be left over after the home loan installment, support expenses and other fluctuated costs; 2) Appreciation - gratefulness can't be depended upon by proprietors of investment property to make their speculations gainful.

A rental is exclusively business and is dependent upon the nuts and bolts of the organic market simply like some other sort of business. Along these lines, you shouldn't have any issues leasing your rental if properties like yours are hard to come by. The facts confirm that openings are your most exceedingly terrible adversary when you are attempting to produce a positive income from your investment property. Opening doesn't create any pay, they just cost you cash. Before you put resources into any investment property you ought to ensure yourself by making an assessment of the rental market.

Check the recurrence of rental postings in your nearby paper and converse with the majority of the rental property professionals and property supervisors in the region that you can. Investment properties close to schools or colleges have more popularity for rentals than others. When you have an investment property you are ready to go, you are not only a financial specialist. So to maintain your business effectively you should be happy to dedicate enough of your time and assets that are fundamental. It is important that you check how much money and time you should spend before you make an interest in an investment property whether you are effectively included every day or you contract a supervisor to maintain the business for you.

Do you live in or around the Outer Banks district? If you do, OK let's say you are looking for an employment change or just a few extra ways to deal with get more income? In case you are and in case you have a bit of money to spend, the extent that startup costs, you may need to consider getting into land business. An uncommon strategy to do that is with the procurement of Outer Banks speculation properties.

Concerning Outer Banks' venture properties, you will find that different properties are joined into the articulation. Though most of us would assume that Outer Bank speculation properties come with multi-family homes or tall structures, they are not really how all Outer Bank venture properties are built. For instance, land that you rent to those with trailers or manufactured homes could be seen as venture property, similarly as business-building spaces. Along these lines, in case you are enthused about buying Outer Banks venture properties to benefit, you may need to look past traditional multi-family homes and tall structures.

Regardless of the way that it is, it is important to understand that you can benefit through the procurement of Outer Banks speculation properties, you may contemplate accurately how the system capacities. If you can find an accessible multi-family home or a skyscraper, a huge part of the work would already be practiced for you. This, however, depends on the condition of the Outer Banks venture properties; you may simply need to make a few minor fixes or updates if any at all. If any updates or fixes are required, when they are done, you can decide to start renting the properties or not. Your leaseholders or occupants will by then pay you an agreed proportion of money on a predestined reason, which is most generally a month to month one.

In case you were enthusiastic about acquiring business Outer Banks speculation properties, you would need to receive a comparable system. In case any updates or fixes ought to be made, you would need to make them before renting out. The primary differentiation between business Outer Banks speculation properties and private Outer Banks venture properties is centered on market.

With business speculation properties you would need to target potential business visionaries, paying little mind to whether those business people need to run a retail store or have a joined office region.

As was referenced above, Outer Banks' venture properties also consolidate lots of lands, which can be rented to those with trailers or manufactured houses. With these sorts of Outer Bank speculation properties, you will always find the startup costs to some degree higher, as you would need to cater to driving force power, water, and various necessities. Regardless, if successfully dealt with, renting pretty much nothing or even gigantic lots of land to the people with trailers or created homes is an unbelievable source of profit.

What is lovely about being an Outer Banks venture property owner is that there is little work required on your part. After you have the property being alluded to arrange for rental you may simply need to do little required fixes here and there. Concerning finding leaseholders or occupants, you will consider this to be a really basic process. Commonly, a fundamental advertisement in one of your local papers is enough to get various responses from potential occupants.

Imagine, instead of working for money that you rather made every dollar work for you 40hrs consistently. Far better, imagine each and every dollar working for you all day every day, for instance, 168hrs/week. Comprehending the best ways you can make money work for you is a critical development made a beeline for wealth creation.

In the US, the Internal Revenue Service (IRS) a government association responsible for social event and approval, groups pay into three wide types: dynamic (earned) pay, simple income, and portfolio pay. Any money you ever make (other than conceivably winning the lottery or tolerating an inheritance) can be arranged as one of these compensation classes. In order to understand how to wind up rich and make wealth, it's essential that you understand how to make various floods of mechanized income.

Crossing point the Chasm

Mechanized income is compensation delivered from a trade or business, which doesn't require the owner to do much. It is routinely adventure compensation (for instance, pay that isn't traversed working) yet not just. The central idea of this sort of compensation is that it could continue whether you continue working or not. As you near retirement you are beyond question hoping to supersede earned compensation with separated, ridiculous compensation. The way to wealth creation earlier on in life is mechanized income; positive pay delivered by assets that you control or have.

One reason people imagine that it's difficult to make the bounce from earned pay to logically detached wellsprings of compensation is that the entire guidance system is in actuality basically planned to teach us to do an obligation and hereafter depend for the most part on earned compensation. This works for governments as this kind of pay produces huge amount of evaluation yet won't work for you on the off chance that your spotlight is on the most capable technique to wind up rich and wealth building. To wind up rich and make wealth you will be required to cross the canyon from relying upon earned compensation so to speak.

Land and Business - Sources of Passive Income

The aloof kind of salary isn't reliant on your time. It is subject to the advantage and the administration of that benefit. Automated revenue requires utilizing different people and group's time and cash. For instance, you could buy an investment property for $100,000 utilizing a 30% initial installment and acquire 70% from the bank. Accepting this property creates a 6% Net Yield (Gross Yield short all Operational Costs, for example, protection, support, property charges, the executives' expenses and so on) you would produce a net rental yield of

$6,000/annum or $500/month. Presently, subtract the expense of the home loan reimbursements of let's say $300/month from this and we land at a net rental payments of $200 from this. This is $200 passive income you didn't have to work or labor for.

Business can be a wellspring of automated revenue. Numerous business visionaries begin in business with beginning a business to sell their stake for somewhere in the range of millions in let's say 5 years time. This fantasy will possibly turn into a reality in the event that you, the business visionary, can make yourself replaceable with the goal that the business' future salary age isn't subject to you. In the event that you can do this, in a manner you have made a wellspring of easy revenue. For a business, to turn into a genuine wellspring of automated revenue it requires the correct sort of frameworks and the correct sort of individuals (other than you) working those frameworks.

At last, since passive income-producing resources are normally effectively organized by you the proprietor (for example an investment property or a business), you have a say in the everyday tasks of the benefit which can decidedly affect the degree of pay produced.

Automated revenue - A Misnomer?

Somehow or another, automated revenue is a misnomer as there is nothing really difficult in being in charge of a gathering of benefits creating pay. Regardless of whether it's a property portfolio or a business you claim and control, it is only very seldom really inactive. It will expect you to be required at some level in the administration of the benefit. Nonetheless, it's uninvolved as in it doesn't require your everyday direct inclusion (or if nothing else it shouldn't in any case!)

To end up rich, consider building utilized/automated revenue by developing the size and level of your system rather than essentially developing your abilities/skill. Purported brilliant people may invest their energy gathering confirmations and testaments, however, well off society invest their time gathering business cards and building connections!

Leftover Income = A Form of Passive Income

Leftover Income is a type of automated revenue. The terms Passive Income and Residual Income are regularly utilized reciprocally; notwithstanding, there is an unpretentious yet significant contrast between the two. It is pay that is produced every once in a while from work done once, for example, repeating installments that you get long after the underlying item/deal is made. Lingering salary is as a rule in explicit sums and paid at customary interims. Some case of remaining pay incorporate:-

- Royalties/profit from the distribution of a book.

- Renewal commissions on money related items paid to a budgetary guide.

- Rentals from a property letting.

- Revenue created in staggered showcasing systems.

Utilization of Other People's Resources and Other People's Money

Utilization of Other People's Resources and Other People's Money are key fixing required for producing automated revenue. Other People's Money gets you time (a key restricting component of earned salary in riches creation). As it were, the utilization of other individuals' assets gives you back your time. With regards to raising capital, organizations that produce passive income, for the most part, pulls in the biggest measure of Other People's Money. This is on the grounds that it is commonly conceivable to firmly inexact the arrival (or if nothing else the hazard) you can anticipate from uninvolved ventures thus banks and so on, will frequently subsidize detached speculation openings. A decent field-tested strategy upheld by solid administration will typically draw in attendant financial specialists or funding cash. Also, land can regularly be procured with a little upfront installment (20% or less now and again) with most of the cash acquired from a bank ordinarily.

Tax breaks of Passive Income

Automated revenue ventures frequently take into account the most ideal expense treatment whenever organized properly. For instance, enterprises can utilize their benefits to put resources into other aloof speculations (land, for instance), and profit of duty reasoning all the while. Also, land can be "exchanged" for bigger land, with duties conceded inconclusively. The expense paid on passive income will shift depending on the person's close to home duty section and corporate structures used. In any case, for the motivations behind outline, we could say that a normal of 20% successful expense on aloof speculations would be a sensible presumption.

In light of current circumstances, passive income is regularly viewed as the sacred goal of contributing and the way to long haul riches creation and riches security. The real advantage of passive income is that it is repeating salary, ordinarily created quite a long time after month without a lot of exertion by you. Building riches and getting to be rich shouldn't be tied to extricating each and every piece of your own vitality, your own assets and your own cash as there is constantly a point of confinement to the degree you can do this. Taking advantage of the viable age and utilization of passive income is a basic advance in making progress toward making money. Start this piece of your money-making venture as right on time as is humanly conceivable for today!

On the off chance that you scan the web for "easy revenue", you may discover a definition or two, however for the most part, what you find are sites attempting to sell you on the automated revenue kind of-the-day. It's disappointing, I know. I don't know about you, but before I bounce into any chance or even before I travel, I like to do my research. That being said, there are a ton of good open doors out there. Be that as it may, before you start burning through cash, we should examine what passive income is and, in particularly, what it isn't.

Webster's dictionary defines automated revenue as "a means of, identifying with, or being business movement in which the speculator does not have quick command over salary". I don't believe that recounts the entire story. Passive income is cash that you get again and again without doing much work (see I didn't say "any work"). It is not quite the same as earned salary, because you are not getting cash for your time (like you would in the case of salary). However, depending on the automated revenue stream that you pick, you may, in reality, have quick command over your salary. However, I'll get to that later.

For what reason would you need automated revenue? All things considered, just as Robert Kiyosaki explained in his book Rich Dad Poor Dad, that is the principle distinction between the rich and white-collar class. The rich put their cash in different automated revenue streams. At the point when their passive income surpasses their costs, at that point, they are monetarily free, "Monetarily free", which essentially implies that you don't need to have normal everyday employment to pay your costs. Furthermore, you are "free" to then do anything you desire!

What Passive Income Isn't

Before I go into revealing to you what passive income is, let me first disclose to you what it isn't. Automated revenue is not the same thing as "leftover salary". Remaining pay is cash that you get in the wake of having done work once. The best model would be the TV sitcoms. A few entertainers get "residuals". On-screen characters get paid for taping the show. A while later, a few entertainers get paid each time the show rehashes. Salesmen that sell administrations, memberships, or sustainable items (like protection) sell that thing once and, giving that the client restores; will get a commission off of every reestablishment. Eminences from the closeout of books and music are also examples of leftover.

Many say that staggered promoting or system advertising deals furnish you with automated revenue. Prepare to be blown away.

On the off chance that you have a private company or are independently employed, regardless of whether you are profiting, this isn't automated revenue. On the off chance that you get compensation from your business, that is earned pay. There is an approach to transform this into easy revenue- so stay tuned.

You know, I need to explain that starting up your own blog cannot be classified as easy revenue. Regardless of whether you are selling an item, (for example, an eBook, course or other data) or an administration, despite everything you need to showcase your site. You should do this paying little mind to whether you are selling your OWN items or reserve the privileges to sell other's items. Showcasing your site is work, it's that simple. In any case, it is anything but a vocation. Furthermore, when your promoting gigs start taking off, you can profit with minimal extra exertion. In any case, that is remaining in my book, not latent.

What Passive Income IS

Passive income is a lot of things. The principal thing that rings a bell, and furthermore, I accept, the most mainstream model are land and property. On the off chance that you acquire a venture property and are getting a positive income from a house, business property, or loft, that is easy revenue. On the off chance that you lease rooms in your home, that is automated revenue as well. You just need to set this up once, and afterward, the pay comes in whether or not you do any work at the end of the month. Premium pay from investment accounts, CDs, and currency market records are latent - the bank pays you for keeping your cash in those records. On the off chance that you have a site with standard advertisements or Google AdSense promotions, that can also be called latent.

If perhaps you put resources into any business, however, don't oversee it, your benefits are viewed as easy revenue, precisely what Webster was thinking when he gave that definition.

Shouldn't something be said about business? Indeed, that relies upon how you set it up. Rich individuals make organizations and set up a framework that the business pursues. That way, if the proprietor travels for a month to Fiji, the representatives pursue the framework and the proprietor still gets the benefits. Any business will obviously begin with a ton of work, however, in the event that you set aside the effort to set up a business so it gets reproducible outcomes (precisely like an establishment), those benefits become uninvolved. What's more, as per the IRS, any payment you get from your business is considered "earned" however benefits are considered "uninvolved". It is crucial when beginning a business to check with a bookkeeper and a lawyer to set up the kind of business that monetarily benefits you the best.

What else can be viewed as easy revenue? What about self-storerooms, parking structures/parts, and cleaners! They all require some opportunity to fire up, however, once they are set up, you gather cash again and again without doing much.

Remaining versus Passive Income

Remaining and automated revenue are closely related. They are both fundamentally the same and a lot of people cannot differentiate them. What does it make a difference, in any case? They are both brilliant approaches to get cash in your grasp quite a long time after a seemingly endless amount of time after month without exchanging your time or your opportunity. How then can it improve than that?

Rude awakening

Be careful with anybody that reveals to you that there is NO work engaged with easy revenue. Passive income does not mean no work! If by any chance you want to invest in a business, a stock, or a land property, you should conduct your research (this is designated "due perseverance"). Research is work! You will likewise be required to deal with your speculations, to determine the status of their advancement and make changes as important. That is work as well!

Fortunately, research and the board are just low maintenance try. What's more, more often than not, that work should be workable from anyplace, incorporating on a shoreline in Fiji.

Let us not overlook the FUN factor. I'm certain there are some of you perusing this who like, even love their employments (on the off chance that despite everything you have one). Some of you have your own business - and well done to you! However, the majority of us are in employments since we have to sustain our families and cover the tabs. Investigating passive income streams and contributing your time and cash can bring you numerous profits. Inquiring about and executing your automated revenue designs with the goal that you can live your fantasies is FUN. Getting cash each month, week, or even each day is FUN. What's more, evaluating new systems and dealing with your cash - when you have some to oversee - is FUN.

I expect that I've carried out my responsibility and given you the passive income nuts and bolts. In the event that you have any inquiries or considerations, don't hesitate to get in touch with me through my site. I'd love to get a notification from you!

The most effective method to Generate Passive Income

A lot of people agree that the way to progress is constancy. They are reluctant to get behind the race. These proactive individuals have demonstrated to wind up a stable in their life. Then again, the languid doesn't have any issue essentially in light of the fact that they don't have anything too. The two kinds of individuals have been so. It sounds reasonable, isn't that right?

Be that as it may, this balance is the relic of times gone by. On the off chance that this is our outlook, we will without a doubt be astounded at the extraordinary fortune of the individuals who have applied less exertion and at the dissatisfaction of the individuals who have put forth a valiant effort. It doesn't imply that life is uncalled for. Actually, we acquire from what we do as well as from what we don't do. The previous is known as dynamic pay; the last mentioned, inactive.

Dynamic salary is a payment we create from our diligent work. When we work for cash, it is a dynamic salary. In any case, when it is our very own cash that works for us, it is known as automated revenue. Passive income is a salary we produce from our venture. Step by step instructions to produce automated revenue without dynamic intercession is certifiably not a sort of enchantment that everybody could have.

How to create easy revenue? Passive income is created when our speculation acquires due to our convenient choice. In this kind of salary, we are paid for the choice we make and for the hazard we take. When we become scared of contributing, we tend not to settle on any choice. Thus, nothing happens to our cash. To produce automated revenue, we should settle on the correct choice on what and when to contribute. We should likewise ascertain the hazard - the higher the hazard, the higher the arrival. The lower the hazard implies the more it takes to get the potential return. It relies upon what our identity is and what venture accommodates our character. Proactive individuals are normally profession inclined so they can effectively produce dynamic pay. Then again, understanding individuals are savvy leaders and daring people.

Presently, the inquiry is what sort of workers we ought to be. Dynamic workers have full control of the amount they could gain, however, there is a limit on the sum as there is the limit in their vitality and time. When they stop, so does their pay. Notwithstanding, uninvolved workers are progressively effective as they appreciate the boundless capability of procuring high with less vitality. Besides, uninvolved workers can be both dynamic and inactive workers. Clearly, passive income is increasingly worthwhile.

It isn't hard to tell how to create automated revenue. There is a great deal of accessible data around us that can enable us to figure out how to start this. We, for the most part, have found out about contribution and among the well known are securities exchange, securities, common assets, protection, annuity plans, and treasury notes. Prior to contribution, it is essential to contemplate your decision venture. We don't need to be the handyman. What is significant is that we comprehend the hazard and the capability of the market we need to enter and start small only for an attempt. As time goes on, we will pick up understanding and will succeed in the market we have picked. In the approach of innovation, it has turned out to be simpler to get more data about any field of undertaking. The web offers various apparatuses we need to end up prepared.

The most essential piece of how to produce passive income is our attitude toward the venture. A few people believe that venture is done so as to continue our day by day need and this is an off-base thought. Provided that this is true, it isn't any greater venture. It is a business. Our quick need must be supported by a dynamic salary. To rely upon speculation for everyday needs is flighty. We should work so as to live and we contribute in light of the fact that we secure our tomorrow. Genuine financial specialists are future situated. They don't actually make cash immediately. In any case, their cash works for them. That is the motivation behind why we call this condition detached. Everyone's need today is not the same as our need later on. Our prompt need is as a result of our quick activity and prompt outcomes cause us to develop. In any case, passive income isn't something that should cause us to develop. This is something that we ought to develop. In this way, whatever we procure now is the thing that we need now. Dynamic salary is the impression of what we do now. The correct frame of mind toward automated revenue is to regard it as a different living element. Dynamic salary is the thing that we need now. Also, passive income is the thing that our venture needs now. It is like a pet that we should raise.

Shouldn't something be said about business? Is it a sort of dynamic pay or detached? As a matter of fact, it is the blend of both. A representative effectively controls his money streams to continue his day by day needs and simultaneously save some greater part for his business as a different element. However, organizations are perplexing these days relying upon their size. Enormous partnerships are for the most part possessed by various individuals called investors. They enlist administrators and even CEO's to effectively control their tasks. Now and again, they intercede on a large scale level. However, their control and exertion are constrained contrasted with the noteworthy pay they get each year if their organizations constantly develop.

For these individuals, these big organizations are their wellspring of automated revenue. For little business people, they should apply all their exertion for their business. They experience difficulty causing their organizations to develop on the grounds that they additionally rely upon the dynamic salary they create from working for their organizations. Would this imply that, in order to create easy revenue, we ought to have had huge funding to contribute? Not really! We can do that by putting resources into portions of stocks even in littler measure of cash. This is likewise valid with shared supports that pool singular interests in modest quantity to make it one major speculation. This implies we produce passive income like huge speculators.

At the time, I didn't have a great deal of cash. In any case, everybody needs to begin some place, isn't that so? My first involvement in this domain, other than enthusiasm on my bank account, was purchasing a sweet machine, filling it with M&Ms and setting up it in the parlor at my fencing club. I determined the expense of a solitary M&M and made sense of what number of M&Ms I would give different fencers for their 25 pennies. Since I at that point knew my overall revenue per deal, I found that I was making a normal $25 every month in passive income subsequent to giving 10% back to the lesser fencing program.

A few people think they are accepting automated revenue when they are really getting the leftover salary. For instance, a protection specialist may win lingering pay as her customers restore their protection approaches. In any case, if the protection operator leaves the organization, that pay leaves.

CHAPTER TWO

WHAT'S A INCOME PASSIVE

Acquiring pay without working is the thing that straightforward pay is about. There are different customary frameworks for extending a straightforward salary. A touch of these systems, everybody considers. Theory property is one approach to manage to get a surge of pay without working. You in a general sense keep up the property and collect the remuneration. It is even conceivable to enlist somebody to oversee and keep up the property so you don't need to do any of the work required for the rental remuneration. There are different wellsprings of basic pay that can be utilized to make two or three floods of compensation and help you to work less and make more.

Legitimately restricting pros are getting straightforward pay when they hand off their work to subcontractors. The subcontractor does the greater part of the work and the legitimate worker is paid a commission for finding the position and enlisting the subcontractors. There is business-related to this kind of robotized salary, at any rate, it is on a very basic level not actually if the concise pro were making every fundamental walk themselves. It comparably enables them to take on more work and accomplish a progressively noteworthy compensation. Right when a temporary master understandings subcontractors to do their work they are not restricted by their own one of a kind capacity to complete the work.

Making a thing that can be sold on the Internet is another wellspring of straightforward pay. Things like electronic books can be sold adequately again and again with essentially the shrouded exertion required to get an anticipated stream of pay. Right when accomplice marketing experts are utilized to sell the thing, the extent of work is even less. In the event that you can get a few of these things available, you will receive an astounding automated pay without lifting a finger.

Redistributing is a remarkable course of action like the concise worker and subcontractor relationship, yet it may be cleaned with different reasons for living. Promoting specialists and visual pros can take on a critical number of more undertakings in the event that they can re-fit the work to different people. This is an amazing way to make a straightforward salary and still work on what you like simultaneously. This fabricates the extent of compensation that can be made by a particular individual.

Contemplating an unprecedented business thought is another approach to manage and produce automated pay. You can establish the course of action to different businesses questioned individuals and convey a pay on their business. This is a perfect utilization of electronic salary. There is no absence of individuals who want to begin another business and on the off chance that you can furnish them with a striking thought and the subtleties for beginning you will have gotten yourself an easy straightforward pay stream.

A robotized salary is basically restricted by your innovativeness. You can evidently think about countless chances to make payments created by others. It is the sharpest thing that a business visionary who is contemplating leaving can do to guarantee that their way of life doesn't change. For specific, authorities there is a relentless cycle of work without get-away or retirement in their future. Passing the work off to another person and up to this point enduring remuneration is the most ideal approach to manage drawing nearer to the day that you can leave. Research the majority of the propensities where you can make automated pay from your repetitive example business. On the off chance that you put your mind to it, there is a huge chance for making payments.

We have always longed to having the decision to do as little as could reasonably be typical and advantage hand over hold hand as the verbalization goes. Who wouldn't be glad to have the decision to secure an enormous compensation with little work required? Clearly if by any chance we could all understand how to be cash tree ranchers we would not have any weights. This would be the ideal modernized pay opportunity, even this would require working up your yield.

To be clear there is likelihood to have a robotized pay opportunity. Truth be told there are a few different ways to deal with this and different others that affirmation they are. This is the whole idea of driving "salary sans work stunts."

One kind of basic salary opportunity that is widely practice is being pay-property cash related ace, is popularly known as being a proprietor. Having adventure property is a sort of a basic salary open passage that has been around for quite a while. While there is some work included and it can also have some valid weight-related with it, being a proprietor is kind of a robotized salary opportunity that isn't all that bad.

There are for every situation new techniques for basic pay openings, which make them accessible. Regardless, the issue is the greater parts of these are ludicrous. In the event that it appears as though it is strange potential results are it is.

Bogus game plans have made out of the likelihood of separated business opportunities. The facilitators of these businesses try to sell the probability that they have a route for you to get rich without making any kind of move or nearby no of anything. They will typically have a smooth little gathering including a course of action of things or they might be based on only a solitary thing.

Notwithstanding, they guarantee that you won't need to do anything as long as you purchase the things and get others to do too. You will by then obtain remuneration according to what everybody you bring into the social event purchases. Also, for everything the individuals they get in addition buy.

This is an awesome idea; even if everything else fails what these people are publicizing is the probability of not attempting to profit. The truth is in any case that these people are attempting to gather people that will purchase from this association with the target that nobody needs to secure. This is a typical example of a basic salary open door that doesn't pass on what it advertizes.

In the event that you need to build a grim commission in a system advertizing business structure, by then you have to understand how to show off the thing to focus on buyers, as opposed to individuals who essentially need to benefit at the push of a catch.

When you search the Internet you are bombarded with a wide range of offers that try to convince you to improve a normal straightforward salary. This should gather that you do work one time and the cash will continue coming in any event, when you rest. In any case, there is a lot of perplexities about what straightforward pay truly is.. You have to understand that there is essentially more to basic pay than just said and overlook it and advantage while you rest. Here are a few pointers to help you fully grasp the real concept of what straightforward pay is.

Understand that work is constantly included:

Motorized pay doesn't mean that you get to only walk around and sit idle while the cash just flows in. You generally have to work to prop up the structure, and then the compensation will as time goes on evaporate. In spite of whether cash was coming in from the earliest starting point that is in light of the way that a colossal measure of work was placed into it toward the beginning stages to get to this point, yet it will take an in every way that really matters the indistinguishable extent of work to support the payment. This is simply cash that is working for you to get you more cash quicker than what you could on the off chance that you had no cash, at any rate, work is consistently included in your region by somehow.

Straightforward salary uses other individuals' time:

Despite what you think about straightforward salary somehow work must be done to bring in the cash. It could mean that you are making each crucial walk while another person makes the basic steps for you. When you can use your cash then that is your cash that is working for you to bring you generally more cash. This can be seen for instance of automated salary, each dollar that you have takes after a little laborer getting you an appearance on the contributed dollar. You can also use cash to use other individuals' as an ideal opportunity to get you more pay. Exactly when the compensation structures are set up you can robotize them with the target that they run snappier or you can pay another person to keep up the framework for you, yet the structure will continue working so as long as it is kept up.

Straightforward salary Is Sustainable:

Overall it is only a structure you have set up that will get cash normally once it is running. You can arrive at the point where it's running so successfully you'll simply deal with the framework to ensure that everything is running smoothly. You should secure at any rate to get the structure in play, when you have the framework you can utilize an impact of the pay that you produce to enlist various individuals to deal with your framework for you. This is affirmed set it and overlook it pay, you're profiting while another person is doing basically everything, on an extremely fundamental level proportionate to what a huge number people accomplish for the affiliation they quit fooling around for every day.

In case you search the web for "robotized income", you may find a definition or two, yet most of what you will find are people endeavoring to sell you on the simple income sort of-the-day. It's confusing, I know. I don't know about you, but before I bob into an opportunity or even before I travel, I like to do my investigation. That being said, there are a lot of good open entryways out there. However, before you start consuming money, we ought to inspect what robotized income is and, most importantly, what it isn't.

Webster's dictionary portrays simple income as "of, relating to, or being business activity in which the examiner doesn't have brief order overcompensation". I don't accept that definition to be the whole story. Simple income is money that you get over and over without doing a great deal of work (see I didn't express "any work"). It isn't exactly equivalent to earned compensation in that you are not getting money for your time (like you would a job). Regardless, dependent upon the simple income stream that you pick, you may as a general rule have fast order over your compensation. Regardless, I'll get to that later.

For what reason would you need a computerized income? Everything considered as Robert Kiyosaki explains in his book Rich Dad Poor Dad, that is the crucial differentiation between the rich and the common laborers. The rich put their money in various computerized income streams. Right, when their computerized income outperforms their expenses, by then they are financially free. "Financially free" just suggests that you don't just have a typical regular work to pay your expenses. In addition, you are "free" to then do anything you want!

What Passive Income Isn't

Before I go into uncovering to you what simple income is, let me initially uncover to you need it isn't. Robotized income is certifiably not a comparable thing as "remaining pay". Remaining compensation is money that you get all the time consequent to having done work once. The best model would be the TV sitcoms. A couple of performers get "residuals". On-screen characters get paid for account the show. A brief timeframe later, a couple of on-screen characters get paid each time the show repeats. Sales reps that sell organizations, participations, or unlimited things (like assurance) sell that thing once and, giving the customer restores, will get a commission off of each reclamation. Eminences from the closeout of books and music are moreover waiting.

Many express that stunned publicizing or framework advancing arrangements outfit you with simple income. Get ready to be overwhelmed. That is staying too.

If you have a private endeavor or are freely utilized, paying little heed to whether you are making huge amounts of money, this isn't robotized income. If you get payment from your business, that is earned compensation. There is a way to deal with change this into computerized income, despite - so stay tuned.

You know, I have to express that starting your own one of a kind site can't be a simple income. Notwithstanding whether you are selling a thing, (for instance, an eBook, workshop or other information) or help, in spite of all that you have to exhibit your site. You ought to do this paying little notice to whether you are selling your OWN things or hold the alternatives to sell other's things. Promoting your site is work, essential as that. Regardless, it definitely not works. In addition, when your displaying tries start taking off, you can make boatloads of money with insignificant additional effort. In any case, that is extra in my book, not disconnected.

What Passive Income IS

Mechanized income is a lot of things. The primary concern that rings a bell, and moreover, I acknowledge the most conspicuous model is speculation property. If you guarantee theory property and are getting a positive pay from a house, business property, or apartment suite, that is robotized income. In case you rent rooms in your home, that is mechanized income too. You simply need to set this up once, and after that, the compensation arrives in an apparently perpetual measure of time after month. Premium compensation from speculation records, CDs, and money market records are uninvolved - the bank pays you for keeping your money in those records. In case you have a site with banner advancements or Google AdSense promotions, that can be called uninvolved as well.

If you put assets into any business, anyway don't direct it, your advantages are seen as mechanized income, unequivocally what Webster was contemplating when he made the definition.

Shouldn't something be said about business? Everything considered that depends upon how you set it up. Rich people make associations and set up a structure that the business seeks after. That way, if the owner goes for a month to Fiji, the laborers seek after the system and the owner still gets the advantages. Any business will clearly start with a lot of work, anyway if you put aside the push to set up a business so it gets reproducible results (correctly like a foundation), those advantages become dormant. In addition, according to the IRS, any payment you get from your business is considered "earned" anyway advantages are considered "unapproachable". It is basic when starting a business to check with a clerk and a legal counselor to set up your business that fiscally benefits you the best.

What else can be viewed as automated revenue? What about self-storerooms, parking structures/parcels, and cleaners! They all require some an opportunity to fire up, yet once they are set up, you gather cash again and again.

Lingering versus Passive Income

Remaining and automated revenue resemble kin. They are both fundamentally the same as and the vast majority truly think about them equivalent words. What does it make a difference, at any rate? They are both great approaches to get cash in your grasp quite a long time after a seemingly endless amount of time after month without exchanging your time or your opportunity. How might it show signs of improvement than that?

Rude awakening

Be careful with anybody that reveals to you that there is NO work engaged with easy revenue. Automated revenue doesn't mean no work! In the event that you will put resources into a business, a stock, or an investment property, you should do your exploration (this is designated "due ingenuity"). Research is work! You will likewise be required to deal with your ventures, to determine the status of their advancement and make changes as essential. That is work as well!

Fortunately, research and the board is just low maintenance attempt. Furthermore, more often than not, that work should be possible from anyplace, incorporating on a seashore in Fiji.

Let us not overlook the FUN factor. I'm certain there are some of you perusing this who like, even love their employments (in the event that regardless you have one). Some of you have your very own business - and congratulations to you! In any case, the vast majority of us are in occupations since we have to bolster our families and take care of the tabs. Investigating easy revenue streams and contributing your time and cash can bring you many, numerous profits. Exploring for and actualizing your easy revenue designs with the goal that you can live your fantasies is FUN. Getting cash each month, week, or even each day is FUN. Furthermore, evaluating new methodologies and dealing with your cash - when you have some to oversee - is FUN.

Easy revenue gotten from an activity or source other than standard business or "work" Communicated another way; it isn't a delayed consequence of trading "working time" for money, for instance, hourly, without fail or month to month remuneration/pay. In this standard circumstance, if you quit working, you quit getting paid! In a mechanized income condition, you keep getting a compensation stream even when you are not viably working. Three ways of creating easy revenue are:

1. You create a book that continues selling long after conveying a greatness stream.

2. You sell an insurance game plan that pays you a commission every month.

3. You create a site that sells various things, each addressing a compensation stream.

Coming up next is a logically complete summary of potential wellsprings of mechanized income.

Annuity portions

Energy on records or other cash related instruments

Sways on a book

Offers of a mechanized/advanced book

Amazing exhibiting pay plans

Stock benefit portions

Rental compensation from endeavor property

Commissions from robotized repeat bargains

Branch commissions

Instructive expense from pre-packaged guidance programs

Online publicizing commissions

Referral rewards

Enrollments or investments

Sweet machine thing bargains

Setting up Passive Income Streams

Since you have a basic understanding of this thought, you may want to explore whether any of the recently referenced passive income openings could work for you.

In keeping an eye on the rundown, an astounding number of these wellsprings of mechanized income can be learned for a reasonable amount of time and moreover money. The five wellsprings of compensation excerpted from the past once-over and showed up underneath may not be feasible for you to look for after in light of the way that they are basically not available to you ie. annuity portions or they would require that you starting at now have a liberal proportion of cash or other budgetary assets. Premium portions, stock benefits, and hypothesis property are occasions of the last referenced. Nevertheless, most of the remaining sources on the summary may be pursuable options depending upon your inclinations, suitability, experience, preparation, etc. Nonavailability of plenty cash spares or other liquid assets need not be a hindrance to making compensation streams from any one of these uninvolved income openings.

As previously explained, the going with wellsprings of compensation openings may not be available or easily understandable for you. However, as you begin to hoard progressively cash related wealth, the premium earned from budgetary records; stock benefits and land theories will become options for you to consider as robotized income business openings.

Annuity portions

Eagerness on records or other cash related instruments

Stock benefit portions

Adventure property pay

Treat machine thing bargains

Your Legacy

One last bit of leeway of setting up standoffish floods of compensation is that they can be passed on to your relatives, accordingly which continues to overhaul your family's lifestyle. It is an overall recognized explanation that passing on the strategies for cash age to your survivors is an essential angle for structure "generational" wealth.

You may be wondering what ways to deal with benefits on the web and how to get rich with kinds of simple income? Or on the other hand, paying little heed to whether there is a "basic robotized income" to be made on the web?

Is it possible to get rich with mechanized income? Is that a certifiable strategy to benefit on the web? Various people may argue that there is such a way to accomplish this when there are such countless ways that can separate you from your money given all of the stunts out there. This article will in a perfect world, grant you a way or two on how to make uninvolved income on the web.

You can benefit on the web and even get rich with it since this is the primary strategy for picking up money that isn't connected to you changing your time for a fixed money total, or what is known as a check. Any kind of mechanized income is, by definition, not appended to exchanging your time for money. Not in the least like a check which is in reality simply trading your time for money, this sort of compensation on the web can empower you to get rich unquestionably in light of the fact that this kind of compensation isn't appended to trading your time anyway relies upon picking up money again and again and in an inert manner which is gotten constantly.

In all honesty, the majority of people online don't benefit from their business. They will never get rich with a benefitting other than unequivocal sorts of non-straight pay that can be created all around with for all intents and purposes zero out of pocket expenses to the individual. Accomplice frameworks to benefit online that can - after some time - structure into computerized income and empower someone to get rich are open from most backup extends on the web. Building an online business and making a solid, standard compensation is most of the time the outcome of wary research, exhibit recognizing confirmation, and real and feasible advancing strategies that produce arrangements and create benefits. Most extraordinary businesses have the online mechanical assemblies, advancement copy and displaying settings to empower partners to succeed and in case they set aside enough money for the task of benefitting on the web, they will succeed. Many, at any rate, watch the accomplishment of some branch sponsors and feel this is an easy way to make robotized income, when in truth, that is far from it.

Auxiliaries who need to benefit through their accomplice ventures working from home can develop different source of income by following the layout spread out for them by the head of the program. Individuals who as of late worked for a check or a liner pay and a short time later understanding that it would not empower them to get rich started an online business that could be attempted to develop an inactive income stream and perhaps more than one. The people who understand robotized income as opposed to straight pay are pulled in to the web to endeavor to make their dreams work out through this medium.

CHAPTER THREE

Important things to note while embarking on a Rental property business

With respect to selling Rental property, there are some insights you may need to consider when dealing in that capacity. The justification is - in the event that you are trying to remove as many parcels as you can from your property, there are sure things you may need to consider in order to increase your odds as a seller. Here we're going to address some noteworthy pieces of selling Rental property which identifies with the territory, motivation, country of your home, and in also important; the expense you will approve of. Consequent to scrutinizing the data given here, you may have the most appropriate appreciation about advancing your property and why all of these perspectives will be basic.

Territory

Understand that area most no doubt had an amazing arrangement to do with the inspiration driving why you purchased your local regardless. Essentially as it was once far-reaching by then, notwithstanding it ends up tremendous when it is an ideal chance to sell. Location has a lot to do with the new buyer's decision basically as the cost where you will detect directly with when the property is sold. Along the line, you'll need to think about the spot when you are preparing your property, organizing within, and evaluating it according to the present market regard.

Motivation

You'll need to ask yourself, 'What is the idea for advancing this property?' Are you slanted to find a way to get your property sold? Is it true that you are going to fight for each nickel and dime or would you say you will be satisfied to gather a few hundred dollars anyplace? Your motivation will at remaining choose if your property gets sold. In the competition that you are not an animated merchant, chances are you'll be gripping that property for an extended time.

Condition

The country of your property is fundamental concerning the excitement of new buyers. Your property should be arranged with the end goal that thinks about the outside, within, the mechanical assemblies, and the kitchen and washroom explicitly. You should thump up the control offer, verify you manage the correct completing, paint the patio each time required, clean or supersede covers as required, paint the inside if fundamental, and ensure that the kitchen and bathroom are in tip apex condition. You'll similarly need to tune in on emptying any chaos that might need to make within the home is by all accounts humbler than it starting at now is.

Cost

Cost will be along these lines as huge as the territory, the thought for selling, and the nation of your home. The expense of your home ought to be established on relative costs inside your zone. Maybe the absolute best techniques to cost your residence will be to talk with a Rental property master that is very prepared about your place and the fluctuating expenses. They will have the choice to assist you with market examples or anything that would conceivably affect charges on a property of your size.

These are only a few among proposals that should be considered when advertising Rental property. In case you are in a locality that you are experiencing difficulty with respect to selling your home, you should pick the option of utilizing a Rental property expert that has a good knowledge of the sort of local where your property is located, and the particular region whereby you mean to sell.

When you rent a room through Rental property, your reputation is in a general sense huge. That is why you need to ensure that the room is totally perfect and alive and well.

Investment property is very empowering stuff. No danger to get around it, this organization is making waves, why? Investment property is a sizeable site intended to inspire renting everything from homes and entire apartment suites to private rooms, barges and yes even close to home islands. There are several thought processes that this organization is jumping on in a critical way, therefore, various people are excited about utilizing it.

For voyagers, spots to keep on being not quite the same as resorts are no ifs, ands or buts a blessing from paradise, as it enables wayfarers to totally evade the cabin business. On the off hazard that you confide in you're the one in one of a kind who has had negative assistance at a cabin, experienced negative sanitation conditions or experienced an extent of wonders, for instance, boisterous rooms, negligent group of laborers or deceiving, you are, clearly, not alone.

Investment property and exceptional districts are taking the increase of this disturbing and have set out to offer voyagers a totally top-notch approach to manage movement lodging. Not amazingly, housing and hotels are vexed and have gone to battle as an instrument for verifying their associations.

The clarification that people love Rental property is that it is as of now feasible to quickly and effectively change your home into a little money machine. Scarcely any people will get rich by methods for utilizing Rental property, anyway, there is doubtlessly a decent course of action of money to be made. Since it is achievable to endeavor and rent a man or lady room, some other world has been opened up to wayfarers wanting to save tremendously on lodging and advance holders planning to create some additional compensation.

A regularly developing number of home loan holders are discovering this probability and the pay that being locked in with the page can bring. In any case, it is important for home loan holders to see that tidiness is a big issue as long as Rental property is concerned. Everything considered buyers can write terrible reviews and discredit your property. On the off risk that your home is messy or ordinarily unpleasant, you will lose customers. Horrendous overviews will value you past all uncertainty as there is a great deal of contention.

The absolute best system to ensure that your household gives unsurprising and reliable assistance and tidiness is to choose a gifted housekeeping organization.

A home holding organization acknowledges quality on how to keep your home as best as ought to be anticipated underneath the conditions. Therefore, you will have the choice to ensure your reputation and save new traffic needing perpetually and a day.

Owning a property isn't basic in view of the constant addition of land costs. As easy as it looks, to rent a property can be irksome and horrendous. There are some elements to consider before acquiring a property. These include the lease rate, the owner's understanding, and the location of the property. You need to initially ask immensely a terrible part every last one of these things before proposing to consent to the arrangement. Set apart some cash to do all these in order to get the magnificent affiliation and the most reasonable detect that you and your family can remain in.

Investigating for each other spot to live in can be basic on the off peril that you do your investigation fittingly. If a rental seems too high for you, have a go at visiting the spot in excess of a couple of occasions over the span of the day, throughout the work week and on a week's end.

When you do this, you will have a conventional idea of the regular exercise schedules of your neighbors while simultaneously watch their condition. In case you are interested in the spot, take anybody with you. It is always reasonable that you don't visit a property for lease alone. This is for your own assurance explicitly in conditions when you are meeting the landowner himself and no longer a Rental property administrator.

Differentiate the property and the region with your lifestyle. In case you have a vehicle, does the space have a garage? If not, will you have a spot to park? Is it found near a bus stop? These are genuine issues you will ask when buying a house. See whether the property is close to your workplace, for the most part, transportation costs will be exorbitant.

When you lease property, think about on consideration what wide assortment of stuff you have. Will they all fit in your new house? On the off risk that you venerate pets or in the competition that you have one, it is impeccable to see whether the landowner permits occupants with pets.

One of the most across the board thoughts in property rental is the standard kingdom of the spot. Check if there are termites or rodents or some various bugs. Regardless of reality that it isn't your obligation to have the apartment suite looking extraordinary, it will be less upsetting for you if you test for damages so the owner will have the alternative to do a couple of fixes before you go in.

One of the most significant focuses is whether you can afford the expense of the contract rate. When you rent property, it is important to observe that not all houses for rent have equivalent rates. The qualification lies generally in the domain and workplaces. Agreeing to the terms of the portion should also be explored. Generally, apartment suite is paid month to month, while others request that they should be paid in advance. Discourse this with the landowner.

To rent a property you should choose a practicable decision. This may likewise potentially be no doubt the hardest want to make. Consider every last one of the great occasions similarly as hindrances of the spot before you do what wants to be finished.

So how does the all-money down technique work by methods for looking for a local with cash? Above all, let me say again that I truly didn't have any cash, on the other hand, I had a great deal of expense from Terry's residential and a couple of houses that I set up to give me significant cash in advance. Banks and residential advance offices a similar will understood money from a home-estimation reserve funds augmentation as cash to purchase a home. On any occasion they did in 1997 underneath the financial standards of the day. What you remember about home credits and advancing is that the guidelines exchange consistently, so this contraption I used in 1997 should maybe have the choice to be used later on. Whether or not it can be used again doesn't really have any kind of effect on me as I acknowledge that there will continually be a means of purchasing Rental property with limited money sooner or later. There will definitely be a way to acquire Rental property yet unequivocally how that will be finished later on I'm not certain beyond a shadow of a doubt.

I started gaining living arrangements in the Mayfair region of Philadelphia with the costs in the $30,000 to $40,000 per home cost go. I would buy a home with three rooms and one bathroom on the second floor with a kitchen; relax zone, and the receiving area on the key floor and a tempest basement. What we call a section home in Philadelphia would contain a porch out the front and a patio the width of the home. Most section houses in Philadelphia are beneath twenty-two feet wide. For those of you who are currently not from Philadelphia and can't picture what a Philadelphia segment residential looks like, I suggest you watch the motion picture

Rocky. Twenty-two properties on each aspect of each square will really determine your ability to be a neighbor. Things that will generally cause a conflict with your Philadelphia neighbors regularly begin from halting, commotion your youths make, the spot you leave your trash can, parties, and the nearness of your home.

In 1998 my better 50% of and I moved in together and to the suburbs of Philadelphia known as Warminster. In the wake of living on a road in Tacony, bounty like Rocky did, I expected to have a space between my neighbor's house and mine. I educated Terry now not to endeavor and think in regards to talking with the people who lived close by to us. I suggested her that that in case one of them comes over with a nutcake I am going to take it and punt it like a football immediately into their porch. I believe I was once encountering the Philadelphia section home issue. My new neighbors in Warminster ended up being amazing people, then again it took me eighteen months before I realized this.

So you simply purchased your domestic line for $35,000 in Mayfair, and after $2000 in shutting charges and $5000 in restoration costs, you get yourself an occupant who wishes to rent the home. Subsequent to leasing the domestic with fine earnings of $200 every month, you now have a tremendous responsibility of $42,000 on your home fee deposit extension that should be paid off. When acquiring the home, I didn't get a home loan as I just bought a home for money as it is stated in the business. All the money I spent on this residence has been spent from the home-value credit score extension.

The cross presently is to satisfy your home-value credit score extension so you can do it once more. We currently go to manipulate an account with your repaired property and tell the domestic mortgage division that needs to do cash out renegotiating of your Rental property venture. It shows that the neighborhood you purchase your property in ought to have a greater sizable scope of estimating as the region of Mayfair did in the mid-90s. The estimating of homes in Mayfair is very bizarre as you would see a $3000 contrast in-home estimations starting with one rectangular then onto the next. This used to be enormous when doing a money-out renegotiating in mild of the truth that it is pretty easy for the financial institution to see that I simply bought my property for $35,000 paying little idea to the way that I did numerous fixes. I should legitimize the way that I've spent greater money on my domestic to set it up, and by placing an occupant in, it used to be currently a recommended bit of Rental property from a task angle.

In the match that I was once lucky like I used to be a long time ago doing this arrangement of acquiring houses in Mayfair and the appraiser would make use of houses a rectangular or two away and return with an examination of $45,000. In those days there had been initiatives enabling a financial specialist to purchase a domestic for 10 percent down or left in as cost doing a ninety percent cash out renegotiate giving me lower back commonly $40,500. Using this gadget enabled me to get back the huge amount of cash I put down on the property. I in fact, paid solely $1,500 down for this new home. For what cause did the domestic loan corporations and the appraisers continue giving me the numbers I needed? I expect in mild of the fact that they wished the business. I would simply recommend the financial institution I want this to come in at $45,000 or I am clearly retaining it financed as it stands. They commonly regarded to give me what I needed sensibly speaking.

This took three to 4 months during which time I can also have spared a couple of thousand dollars. Between the money I spared from my undertaking and my speculations and money out renegotiating, I had recharged most or the majority of my assets from my home-value credit score extension that used to be presently zero, to begin with. Furthermore, that is simply what I proposed to do. I utilized this framework to buy four to six properties a year using a similar cash to purchase home after homes and more again. In actuality, the approach is a no-cash down or minimal expenditure down procedure. At the time I had $60,000 in reachable belongings to use to buy houses off of my HELOC, so I would purchase a home and afterward renew the cash. It used to be an awesome means that was once legitimate, and I could picture my dream of being a Rental property monetary expert becoming a reality, even though I wasn't there yet.

During the years from 1995 to 2002, the Rental property showcase in Philadelphia made innovative increments of possibly 6 percent as every 12 months went by. I began to observe my properties that used to be 100 percentage value, which ability I had no exclusive types of speculations to see when computing my complete assets. As a rule, the initial five years of my Rental property vocation turned out poorly in light of the lousy selections I made shopping for buildings and the decrease in the market. Moreover, my absence of gaining knowledge of and involvement in fixes made it unpleasant. The second five years of my Rental property vocation that I truly have done the manner of clarifying didn't get a lot of money go with the flow either. I bolstered myself essentially through my vocation as an income rep, alternatively I may want to apprehend what would be inevitable that not some distance off Rental property would have been my full-time gig.

Realty Professionals of America

I declare a vicinity of enterprise that has a Rental property organization as someone referred to as Realty Professionals of America. The organization has a remarkable association where another operator receives 75 percentage of the commission and the agent receives simply 25 percent. On the off risk that you don't have any acquaintance with it, this is a quite first-rate arrangement, especially for any other Rental property specialist. The organization additionally presents a 5 percentage sponsorship charge to the specialist who patronize them on every arrangement they do. In the event that you convey a man or woman who is a rental property professional in to the employer that you have supported, the professional will pay you a 5 percent sponsorship out of the representative's end so the new real property agent you supported can achieve seventy-five percentage commissions. Notwithstanding the abovementioned, Realty Professionals of

America offers to construct the rental property professional's bonus by means of 5 percent subsequent to accomplishing mixture fee benchmarks, up to a restriction of ninety percent. When a commission benchmark is arrived at, an operator's bonus fee is maybe diminished if commissions in the subsequent year do not arrive at a lower gauge sum. I as of now hold 85 percent of each and every one of my arrangements' bonuses; in addition to that, I get sponsorship assessments of 5 percent from the commissions that the operators I supported procure. On the off threat that you'll like to become familiar with becoming part of the Realty Professionals of America's incredible arrangement, it would be perfect if you call me immediately on 267-988-2000.

Getting My Rental property License

Something that I did in the late spring of 2005 in the wake of leaving my all day occupation was once to make preparations to get my Rental property permit. Getting my Rental property permit used to be something I continuously needed to do but never seemed to have the time to do it. I'm sure you have heard that a thousand times. Individuals constantly say that they will accomplish something soon as they discover a chance to do it, then again they never seem to discover the time, isn't always that right? I do whatever it takes now not to give myself excuses about why I shouldn't do important things. So I've determined earlier than I at any point left my all-day work that one of the primary matters I would do was to get my Rental property permit. I joined up with a college referred to as the American Rental property Institute for a fourteen-day full-time program to gather my permit to promote Rental property in the territory of Pennsylvania. Two wonderful people with a universe of experience taught the class, and I was happy about the time I spent there. Following finishing the route at the American Rental property Institute, I booked the following reachable day supplied through the kingdom to take the kingdom test. My instructors' advised me to take the check following the type ended up being an exceptional proposal. I finished the check decisively and have utilized my permit ordinarily to purchase Rental property and minimize the costs. In case you want be a full-time Rental property monetary specialist or a commercial enterprise Rental property speculator, at that factor you should get a permit. While I know a couple of persons who don't accept this, I'm convinced it's accepted by a majority.

I took a shot at one association at $3 million the fixed fee to the purchaser's Rental property operator used to be $75,000. When my provider took an offer, I left with $63,000 commission on that one alone. With the rate each and every time of being an actual estate expert running about $1200 each and every year, this one association on my own would've paid for my Rental property permit for fifty-three years. Also, the number of incidental advantages like approaching the numerous posting administrations supplied an excessive wide variety of real property sellers in this nation. While there are distinctive methods to gain admittance to the range of posting administrations or another application like it, a Rental property permit is a brilliant approach.

Some of the negatives I hear about having your Rental property allow is the way that you need to unveil that you are real property professional when buying a domestic in case you are speak me to yourself. Maybe I'm missing something, but on the other hand, I do not think about this to be a negative thing. In case you're talented in the distinctiveness of exchange, it's, in reality, one more obstacle that you need to manage. I understand you may want to wind up in a claim where a court could accept in light of the fact that you are real property agent you need to be aware of each one of these things. I do not go through my time on earth agonizing over the million distinctive ways I can be sued anything else than I stress over getting hit by way of an automobile each time I pass the road.

CHAPTER FOUR

Analyzing a rental property

Enthused about profiting by Rental property anyway scanning for an alternative rather than agreements, dispossessions, inhabitants, or flipping Rental property? Gaining the benefit to assemble on criminal Rental property charges can be an advantageous theory even with confined capital.

All things considered, assess charges on Rental property to owners consistently and consider portion by a particular date. The bills are assessed depending on property estimation and can keep running from two or three hundred dollars to a couple of thousand dollars. If they are not paid when due they become criminal and the area can charge interest. In various states, the areas are allowed to dole out their privilege to assemble the bad behavior to an examiner.

When the property owner pays the toll to the area, the examiner immediately gets their basic endeavor notwithstanding the interest. The reasonable interest varies by zone running between 5-18 percent for every annum all around. If a property owner fails to pay the fine within the time allocation, the examiner can begin methods to seize the property. Evaluation liens generally take need over all other property commitments, including contracts.

Before causing the endeavor through and through to explore the property to certify it is appealing and to sidestep any issue properties. Be certain the estimation of the property far outperforms the locale obligation bill. A general standard rule is a property estimation at any rate on different occasions the aggregate owed.

It is basic to comprehend that the strategy and systems will move fundamentally by zone and that not all states look into cost lien bargains. Moreover, remember that there is a difference between evaluation lien verifications and obligation deeds. Control and obligation regarding property is only possible through an obligation deed after any predefined recuperation period has ended.

For example, in Orange County, Florida obligations become criminal for non-portion April 1 of the following year. The area by then conveys the leeway of announcements in the paper during the extended length of May.

A kind examiner can enlist to offer on the supports at a deal. Rather than an "up close and personal" auction, the offering now occurs on the web. Bidders must store 10% of the aggregate they plan to proceed with the area. Orange County can charge 18% on delinquent evaluations so the offering starts at this most noteworthy and is offered down. So a bidder ready to secure 10% would persuade a bidder needing 12%.

A triumphant bidder pays the zone for the proportion of delinquent obligations and obtains their appearance when the bill is paid by the property owner (the territory keeps the qualification in eagerness between the total accumulated and the money related pros winning offer). Budgetary pros owning supports that have not been paid or recovered by the owner for a period of two years are qualified to apply for an obligation deed bargain. The greater part of property owners deals with their delinquent tab before it goes to the deed compose. This empowers theorists to secure strong returns upheld by means of Rental property. Right when an owner fails to pay, it is serviceable for a budgetary pro to guarantee a property worth a large number of dollars for a theory of just two or three hundred dollars with much greater benefits available for resale.

This present downturn of 2008 to 2010 has really destroyed the protections trade which has compelled various individual budgetary masters to reevaluate their needs. A significant part of these monetary authorities is starting to look for elective kinds of contributing, one of which is Rental property.

I know there's been a hotel showcase crisis that has mirrored the money related trade crisis from various perspectives, anyway the truth remains that right now may be a perfect chance to get into Rental property contributing. Expenses have dropped altogether, once in a while as much as 30 or 40% on properties regardless of what you look like in practically every region in America. That is my technique for uncovering to you that there are some amazing courses of action to be had right now which just pledges to give indications of progress as time goes on.

Today I have to examine two or three ways to deal with profit by the present Rental property contributing condition and give you a couple of things to focus on that you probably won't have thought of on your own.

Today likely the best detect that we're seeing to place assets into Rental property incorporates different family structures with up to 10 units. It's optimal to place assets into these different family structures just in towns that you starting at now live in. Do whatever it takes not to buy a couple of these scattered the country over in light of the way that with our present economy they may take more thought and greater affirmation on your part to get them up and productive which means owning one in the town you currently live in is going to make things considerably progressively easy for you, in any occasion until further notice.

The mind-boggling favorable circumstances of these sorts of hypotheses are that they're minimal enough to be supervised by the owner, you. One thing you're obviously going to need is to examine before you purchase the available laws with respect to these sorts of structures.

Various towns have rent control laws similarly as non-removing laws that make it fundamentally progressively difficult for you to discard tenants that aren't paying rent. Without a doubt, this may be the explanation the present owner has had so a lot of issues that they have to sell. You can't make an advantage if your inhabitants don't pay their rent and you can't expel them without consuming a considerable number of dollars in authentic costs and various extensive stretches of time.

However, in case you can find one of these speculation properties in your general region and there aren't any unpleasant laws that would impact you, by and by may just be the perfect time to swoop in and get it. Do whatever it takes not to be humble about offering ridiculously low expenses in light of the way that various money related experts are planning to sell at any expense to get out from under their home credits.

A lot of people obtained the properties with variable or movable rate home loans back when things were great and are presently finding that they can't renegotiate those advances because of the present condition of the economy and the present condition of the financial market.

This is your opportunity to benefit in Rental property, notwithstanding during a downturn.

With the current money related issues the manner in which it is, speculations are searching down for financial specialists around the world. Financial exchanges are not working out quite as well, neither are the assets which contribute there. Gold has turned out to be too costly to even think about purchasing as are numerous different assets. That doesn't leave speculators numerous spots to get a decent return. With the exception of one kind of venture, the well established ensured approach to get an arrival - Rental property.

Customarily Rental property has been probably the most secure speculation, particularly long haul. There is constantly a need for lodging, and regardless of current money related markets, your venture is constantly protected and will quite often increase. Obviously when we talk Rental property speculations, a lot of people will think about the family home, however, there is more cash to be made in this industry.

The most popular method by which individuals profit in Rental property is by buying the home or condo and renting it out to others for a charge every month. Presently this might be to keep tenants which are considered, more secure as the month to month rental expense is increasingly steady. Or on the other hand, for lofts or homes in prevalent visitor goals, there is a rental charge for each night or week. This sort of occasional settlement will prompt a lot higher expenses, yet this may not be as steady, particularly on account of some down times (for example, winter in certain areas).

The two regular strategies where individuals pay for Rental property speculations are follows. For those with a lot of fluid money, they may possess the property through and through. These recoveries will mean that any rental payment is coming directly into your pocket. Anyway for other people, who don't have the capital or wish to possess many occasion homes, different banks and individual credits can be utilized to buy the property. With these advances one may pay the 'contract' during each time with the rental pay (as this will diminish the interest you pay). Others utilize the idea of an interest just credit, which is the situation where they just pay the interest of the advance and never any of the head. In this circumstance, the arrival on venture comes when the time has come to sell the Rental property. You should be cautious about this kind of credit and be certain the property cost will build every year with a higher rate than the interest you pay.

Regardless of how you choose to pay for Rental property speculations, be guaranteed, they are an extraordinary cash creator. On the off chance that you take a look at a portion of the independent moguls around the globe, you will see something they all have in common. They profited in land ventures and property improvement. Frequently beginning with one property these insightful financial specialists make such exceptional yields that before long, they are already controlling numerous properties and even their own high rise structures. Start your adventure today and put resources into land to make a benefit.

Numerous individuals are thinking about venture realty to have something they could get cash from. It is tied in with making benefits that you also can get yourself into. Step into the Rental property business world and produce proceeding with income with realty venture.

No degree or any instructive accomplishment is required to have realty for speculation. All you need is capital and the correct information, which you can acquire without attending a school. Appropriate learning on realty speculation can be gotten any place you are, even at home as long as you most likely are aware where to get supportive data or courses on the web.

As a potential realty financial specialist, it is important for you to figure out how you can diminish all costs included and boost your income. You need to survey related issues like the rental rate, rental payments, property fix costs (current and future use), profit that you can get in the event that you sell your property and quantifiable profit.

Starting in speculation realty isn't very easy. Discovering venture realties can be testing however, with the correct skill, appropriate instruction, key arranging, and compelling techniques, you can clearly deal with and manage nearly everything without problems. On the off chance that you are longing to produce proceeding with stream of money with realty, try to stay up with the latest with the most recent patterns in realty venture and what can be normal later on.

Also, you need to discover exactly how you can build up an incentive with a speculation realty that you can control. Other than purchasing a limited realty, there are numerous different things that you should consider aside low market worth cost. Numerous realty financial specialists are thinking about dispossessed homes that they can embellish and sell at a market worth cost.

In spite of the fact that dispossessed realties can be an achievable venture, despite everything you must be cautious in deciding their good and bad times as now and again, these properties can just cost you more. A large number of these properties require costly fixes and exorbitant remodels. Being a financial specialist, you need to perform assessments either without anyone else or with an expert at that point to gauge the expenses that might be associated with improving the property.

You also need to make sense of when you can anticipate an arrival on speculation. On the off chance that you picked realty will just motivate you to continue going through for a year as opposed to picking up inside three or four months, discover venture realty and consider different methodologies that can give you incredible benefits.

You need an operator who is known and who acts rapidly for your benefit. For instance, will they show your property quickly if a purchaser needs to see it? The operator, who sold me the property I currently live in, wouldn't show me around it for 48 hours as he was too busy... When I advised the seller - she happened to cut the garden at the front of the property and I halted to talk with her - she was angry with him. She was paying him all that commission and he wouldn't set aside the effort to show a purchaser round in an auspicious way. I don't know whether he is still in business however, there are some brilliant models that I can discuss having encountered them with the operator who sold me that house.

Most importantly, he was a liar. He advised the merchants that they needed to go out while he held an Open House for imminent purchasers. I happened to drop by after the Open House and I saw that no one had gone to his Open House, yet he told the dealers that individuals came to the Open House.

With this specific arrangement, I was conflicted with my very own recommendation of never being the principal individual to name a cost. I was so amped up for the property, that I offered a significant amount at the start. After the arrangement was finished the operator revealed to me that no one else would have offered such a significant amount for the property. I felt terrible. Be that as it may, in a resulting exchange with the merchant, he made me feel somewhat better by saying from my point of view, I think you got a lot. From your point of view, you think you paid a lot for the property. Be that as it may, it was a great learning background. Try not to be the first to name a cost, do your exploration, yet even as the purchaser or the dealer, attempt to arrange a superior cost.

As the dealer, know that in the event that you have given the specialist time limits for him to be the sole operator before it goes on a numerous posting, they are regularly edgy to make a deal with the goal that they don't need to part their bonus. So regardless of whether they have done due industriousness, they are still prone to guide you to bring down your cost by 10% or 20% to get individuals keen on coming, and after that attempt to constrain you into selling route underneath the value you needed to acknowledge. Presently, when it goes on the open market, in a decent economy your specialist probably won't try too hard to find you a purchaser. In a poor economy, they might be frantic enough to take the necessary steps to get you a purchaser, including utilizing harassing strategies to get you to bring down your asking cost. They don't stop for a second to think about the fact that on the off chance that you don't sell it at this value, you might clutch it for an extensive stretch of time. In the event that you do offer it at a much lower value, we'll have a greater amount of a chance to sell it for you.

A customer of mine was convinced to sell her home at closeout. She truly didn't know whether she needed to go that course, however, the operator persuaded her that she could presumably go anyplace from $525K to $585K for her home - that it would be a speedy deal, she would get her cash, it would be finished. Spent over $5K on publicizing which the operator had coercively proposed, and after that the day preceding the property was to go to sell, the specialist called her and advised she expected to set her save cost at $450K and that she was even lucky she got that.

This is such a gross absence of trustworthiness. They do this constantly. At no time when he was forcing her to put her property up at sale did he reveal to her that she would likely need to lose $130K. She accepted it with little or no evidence that she would leave the arrangement with a benefit. Rather, on the off chance that he had his way, he would have gotten the commission and she would have continued the misfortune. She came to me directly after the operator called her advising her to decrease her asking cost. She was in tears since she had just found another property believing that she would have the cash from the closeout of this house. I prompted her not to proceed with the bartering. So when she went in there that same night and disclosed to them she wasn't proceeding - they said, "God help us, you can't do that." Also, she stated, gracious yes I can, you're not getting my mark thus you can't sell my home.

Remember that agents make their living from bonuses on deals. The commission depends on a level of the deal cost and is determined on a recipe the operator ought to unveil in many nations, in the event that you inquire. Like everything else in Rental property, it is debatable! Talk about the commission before making or accepting an offer.

The best time to talk about the commission is the point at which the gatherings are near the point that it is just the commission that is standing out. Remember, agents are especially eager in the downturn market, and multiple times out of ten it fills in as they would very much want to sell a property and make some commission than let the deal fall through and make nothing.

To summarize:

- guarantee that your Agent will show your property in an auspicious way if a forthcoming purchaser turns up

- Attempt to get suggestions for an operator who has uprightness and who is straightforward

- don't be rushed and don't get scared. It's your property; you're the one in control. Eventually, somebody will purchase your home.

CHAPTER FIVE

How to set the right price for your Rental property listing

Having your own house is an extraordinary and enabling accomplishment. This is the reason people who don't have one imagined some time or another of purchasing their very own homes one day. At the point when that opportunity arrives, the dream is currently a reality, yet it is presently the journey with respect to where your dream home ought to be. Finding the correct spot for your home possesses become the following huge energy for you.

Since you have chosen to purchase a home, choose what amount it should cost. Expertise huge the house ought to be and in the event that you need a huge grass or not. Set it recorded as a hard copy of how much your home should cost you. Be reasonable and don't overrate or undervalue your dream home. This is the place "realizing what you truly need" is significant. It is your dream home. Thus, it ought to be something other than what you need.

To be progressively exact, you should initially know where your home ought to be. You can pick the present city you live in as the location for your home. It is completely up to you. Consider the area dependent on your inclination: do you appreciate city life or the calm nation? In the wake of comprehending what you truly need, you would now be able to begin searching for that ideal spot. This will likewise rely upon the amount you can bear the cost of as costs of parts in the city could cost significantly more than parcels in the nation.

House and parcel bundles are the most suggested alternative for would-be property holders. This spares you the time and stress from procuring modelers and contractual workers for structure and development. The drawback is that you have a home where you needed to live, however, you may wind up with a home that didn't coordinate with what you envisioned it to be. Subdivisions are well known with house and part bundles, yet additionally consider Rental property properties, which have extraordinary areas in urban communities that are available to be purchased. So cautiously think about this before settling on an official conclusion.

Searching for the ideal area for your dream home could take some time, yet it will be justified. The land where your dream house will be part of your home so set aside the effort to locate the ideal rental property parcel that where your own haven ought to be. Your spending limit likewise influences where that land is located. As we said earlier, lands in the city will cost more than lands in small towns.

Obviously whoever is hoping to sell a house is definitely going for the most elevated offer. Be that as it may, this isn't generally the most ideal approach, from the merchant's point of view. There are different interesting points other than the cost when you're hoping to sell your home.

You may be amazed by what you've recently perused previously. It's very regular; we as a whole need to make the best out of any arrangement, particularly when selling our home. Anyway, this isn't generally the sharpest course for a merchant to take.

However, you have to contemplate some huge perspectives before setting up an extremely high selling cost. Enlisting a rental property professional can be an answer to a ton of situations you may have.

Sure going through some extra money on a Rental property specialist doesn't sound so incredible. In any case, when you realize he will bring you nothing else but an extraordinary safe lawful arrangement, you ought to reexamine hiring a rental property professional. The vast majority are typically disheartened by the expense most rental property agents charge, yet most rental property professionals are constantly worth that little expense.

Above all else, setting an excessively significant expense can just push a ton of buyers away. Then again, approaching a lower-than-should-be cost for your home can't in any way be to your advantage. Perhaps the hardest part about selling Rental property is deciding the perfect cost, so you attract genuine purchasers without missing out on potential cash.

As you see, you have to build up some sort of harmony between the two wrong costs and concoct the correct one. A rental property agent can truly come in handy with regards to deciding the correct beginning selling cost for a house, in view of his experience in the field. The worth which they are giving you is much worth their expense. They will have the option to rapidly offer your home to a certified purchaser, without having you pass up on a great deal.

He is definitely no stranger to the house selling business sector costs in the region your house is situated. You will need to set an aggressive cost for your home since you wouldn't need any potential purchaser to turn their head and turn away subsequent to seeing your "available to be purchased" sign.

Realizing a reasonable selling cost for comparable properties in your general vicinity will sure guide you for making a sensible offer. Make a point to set up littler costs in the event that you plan on selling the house quickly.

When selling a property, probably the greatest thing you need to think about is setting the selling cost. Set it excessively high and you could frighten potential purchasers off. Set it excessively low and you end up not getting the best an incentive for your speculation. So how would you approach setting the correct sticker price for your property? One thing that could help you is a similar market examination or CMA.

A CMA is an archive that could differ from a two-page to 50-page report. This would incorporate a few assume that would enable you to choose the correct cost for your home. Fundamentally, a CMA contains your opposition as these are Rental property properties that are in the market or have been there as of late.

When scrutinizing a CMA, you would see a lot of information. In setting a cost for your home, there are sure gatherings that you should take a gander at. First of all, the gathering of sold postings would give you an awesome thought about how many houses are being sold for in the market as of late. This would give you a decent beginning stage in deciding the sticker price that you would put on your property before you make it available to be purchased.

The subsequent stage for you to take is to discover comparative properties with the goal that you can get a decent correlation. For instance, deciding the present market price for your one-story house would be hard in the event that you just contrast it with a three-story property. That said let us take a look at what you should search for in a property to contrast with your home.

One of the main things to search for is properties that have a comparable area as your property. Appraisers generally put together their last figures with respect to this and it merits remembering that bigger square-foot homes are normally worth not exactly what littler square foot houses would.

Something else is the age of the house. Since models in development and the character of houses change with time, it is significant that you contrast your property and as of late sold ones that are constructed inside a couple of long periods of yours. This would give you a superior thought regarding the value that your home would order in the market.

When playing out a Comparative Market Analysis (CMA) to decide the asking cost before you sell your home or apartment, the typical path is to take a look at the latest practically identical deals. In any case, consider the possibility that there are no tantamount deals. Consider the possibility that a townhouse complex or neighborhood is generally little and there is almost no turnover of the properties. How would you gauge the present market estimation of a property you wish to sell when nothing around you has sold for a long time or more and costs have gone up or down fundamentally?

An inquiry came up over supper with certain companions an evening or two ago regarding how you would explain this evaluating difficulty. My companions have a townhouse in Complex GC, an inside unit that has been pleasantly refreshed. Since the last deal in their complex happened almost 2 years back, and costs have changed a considerable amount since 2005, this was going to take some work. One thought that struck us was to utilize the market information from other apartment suite deals close by networks that are of comparable quality and square so as to extrapolate an expected equitable price for their property.

The technique I used to guesstimate the present honest estimation of their property included doing broad unit by unit deal correlations for as far back as five years of the properties sold in 3 other close location that I will allude to as TC, WM, and MT. By assessing different units that were comparative in area, number of rooms, washrooms, area, and other applicable highlights, I had the option to adopt a chronicled strategy to deciding relative qualities for the properties that sold. Taking a look at 5 years of offers information I endeavored to scientifically extrapolate verifiable varieties in value per square foot and the connections between comparable quality units in every unpredictable.

The explanation behind returning 5 years was to guarantee that the information is utilized to extrapolate a present honest cost for Condo GC considered whatever number pertinent deals as could reasonably be expected over a significant stretch of time. This smoothed out any value abnormalities that may have happened with individual deals. Anyone specific deal may be a deal or overrated in relative terms, dissecting 5 years of information limited those loopholes.

The authentic information demonstrates that condos in TC sell in a range that is between $80 per square foot to $100 per square foot more than comparative quality apartment suites in the GC complex. It is to some degree uncommon that this value difference can be extrapolated dependent on dollars per square foot instead of a differential dependent on a level of authentic deal costs. Ordinarily, one would expect that there would be a predictable rate differential as opposed to a dollar differential when contrasting units between the two edifices. There were insufficient deals in edifices MT or WM over the multi-year time frame to bring about any huge information that would influence the appraisals being made.

It gives the idea that the essential explanation that condos in TC sell at a greater expense for every square foot are because basically the majority of the units have carports, the properties are more current in development and the complex has broad courtesies including a pool, tennis courts, spa, clubhouse, practice room, and other basic territory offices, when contrasted and the comforts for Condo GC. Different components that one must consider when playing out this kind of investigation include the area of the unit in the complex and whether a property is an inside unit or an end unit. In the event that updates have been played out that would surely have increased the value of any property and this can shift significantly all around.

The latest offers of updated units in TC have been from $492 per square foot up to $524 per square foot. This would demonstrate a present equitable incentive in Complex GC, for comparable quality apartment suites, in the scope of $412 to $444 per square foot dependent on the verifiable value differential of $80 to $100 per square foot and how widely a unit has been overhauled. Excellent overhauls all through can have a colossal effect by the way you value property available to be purchased.

One other significant factor to consider is that an inside unit will commonly sell for not exactly an end unit of similar quality. It's only an unavoidable truth that most apartment suite proprietors in Village and other retreat networks need an end unit and are happy to pay a premium for one.

For single-family private deals this procedure is a hell of much increasingly confused, particularly in a place like Lake Tahoe where there are no tract homes and for all intents and purposes each house is extraordinary. Get the job done it to state that you can't simply take a look at what the neighbor's place sold for.

Nobody can say without a doubt if this examination is the most ideal approach, as it is a ready purchaser and an eager dealer that will eventually decide the genuine equitable cost for any property. It does anyway give one approach to taking a look at evaluating how to value your property available to be purchased when there is no similar deals information to depend on. Regardless of whether a specific market is hot or cold it has a great deal of stock or is just months from the bustling selling season (as is commonplace of resort markets), there are numerous elements that will influence the ebb and flow market estimation of any property. In a Rental property market, for example, Incline Village where there are for the most part custom homes and moderately couple of exchanges on a yearly premise, evaluating a property available to be purchased can be a confounded and interesting procedure.

One reason I appreciate selling Rental property in Incline Village and Crystal Bay is that it furnishes you with these sorts of difficulties all the time. Each home and apartment suite available to be purchased in Incline Village that I get the chance to see is novel here and there and until an arrangement closes escrow you never truly recognize what the honest estimation of a specific property genuinely is.

The strategies and date portrayed thus don't comprise a conventional examination or way to deal with doing property evaluations and is not understood accordingly. This article depicts one approach to attempt to gauge equitable worth dependent on a relative market examination utilizing information from the neighborhood MLS and the writer's involvement in an interesting retreat showcase. The creator is an authorized Rental property operator, not an authorized Rental property appraiser. The techniques suggested above are for scholarly discussion and not intended to substitute for an expert examination. The best way to get a precise gauge of the honest estimation of any property is to contract at least 1 authorized appraiser in your State and have a total evaluation performed of the subject property.

Despite the fact that getting as much benefit out of selling your home seems like the objective, it isn't generally the best practice. Some of the time the best deals cost to put on your house isn't generally the best.

This may appear to be unnatural to you. Obviously we as a whole need to get much cash-flow as could be expected when selling our home. Yet, first, you have to choose what the objective of your deal is and how practical the cost we are inquiring.

Employing a rental property professional to help you in selling your home can be a good move. A rental property agent can enable you to explore the way toward deciding your asking cost. Your rental property professional can enable you to contemplate all viewpoints for setting your business cost. It really makes life a mess simpler to hire somebody who can take a large number of the cerebral pains related to searching for lofts off your back.

It might seem pointless to pay a commission to the Rental property operator from part of your benefit, but truth is that your rental property professional can guarantee you have a smooth and lawful selling procedure. Your rental property professional could likewise get their bonus on the off chance that they help you locate the most noteworthy bidder and give you different tips on the best way to get that asking cost.

A rental property professional can be your best device in setting the correct cost at which to list your home. Your rental property agent's involvement with selling, advertise investigation and working with buyers can be priceless.

The most significant thought is the present lodging business sector costs in your general vicinity. Your rental property professional will be conversant with the market and can enable you to decide the most focused cost at which to list your home.

It is likewise critical to think about how rapidly you have to sell your home. If you are in a rush to get out from under your present home loan, consider setting your business cost under normal market esteem. Something else, realizing the normal selling costs for comparable properties in your neighborhood is the most ideal approach to set your posting cost and sell your home in an auspicious way.

The initial introduction factor in Rental property is a major ordeal creator. Commonly the initial introduction is more powerful than a point by point investigation of the home. We've all known about 'Love at first sight.' We know it's only a cliché, however, underneath a great deal of alleged 'idioms' is a piece of truth. Individuals work from feelings most of the time. Either intentionally or subconsciously, we get an impression about things that trigger either positive or negative sentiments towards it.

When you assume the job of a dealer, you need to comprehend the significance of initial introductions. On the off chance that the buyer gets a terrible early introduction, your odds of selling are decreased by a major edge. There are a couple of spots where you can improve the initial introductions of your home, and it's a gainful exercise for you:

The first and most clear region is the day that the potential purchaser visits the home to see it firsthand. When they drive up your road they start to shape their feelings toward the neighborhood. Supposing that they buy, they'll be driving up this road. They take a look at the house you're selling, and also at the houses around it. That is the reason neighbors are so critical to home estimation. Your home should rate among the best ones that exist in that area, except you are buying due to a low price tag.

A few things you ought to do before the home visit, evacuate dead plants, rake leaves, cut grass, and tidy up the home. The carport is probably the greatest purpose of early introduction. On the off chance that they like driving into your garage, it will establish an extraordinary pace for the house. Simply put yourself in the buyer's shoes, and consider what you'd like to experience.

One region that some don't consider appropriate off lies with the photos you take for publicizing your home. These photos should be top quality and expert. . On the off chance that your house is recorded there, it should be exhibited in the same class as it very well maybe. Furthermore, you ought to have the option to give the searcher the same number of various looks as they can get, so they feel from their hunt that they genuinely comprehend what the home resembles.

When you attempt to make sense of the approaching cost for your home, don't be in reverse about asking companions. What's more, don't be immediately affronted by amicable analysis. Simply accept it for what it's worth and realize that various individuals respond differently to specific circumstances. What's more, this is the manner through which it will go with planned buyers. So approach it with a receptive outlook, and check whether you can improve anything to change any negative criticism.

www.ingramcontent.com/pod-product-compliance
Lightning Source LLC
Chambersburg PA
CBHW030639220526
45463CB00004B/1582